THE PSYCHOLOGY OF PROCRASTINATION

THE

Psychology of Procrastination

UNDERSTAND YOUR HABITS,
FIND MOTIVATION,
AND GET THINGS DONE

HAYDEN FINCH, PHD

ROCKRIDGE
PRESS

For general information on our other products and services or to obtain technical support, please contact our Customer Care Department within the United States at (866) 744-2665, or outside the United States at (510) 253-0500.

Rockridge Press publishes its books in a variety of electronic and print formats. Some content that appears in print may not be available in electronic books, and vice versa.

Cover Designer: Jay Dea
Interior Designer: Lisa Forde
Art Producer: Sara Feinstein
Editors: Samantha Barbaro and Brian Sweeting
Production Editor: Matthew Burnett
Production Manager: Jose Olivera

Illustrations used under license from iStock.com.

Author photograph courtesy of Nicole Thomas Photography

ISBN: Print 978-1-64739-823-1
eBook 978-1-64739-496-7
R0

Introduction and How to Use This Book

YOU'VE STRUGGLED WITH PROCRASTINATION FOR YEARS. In fact, for as long as you can remember, you've had trouble meeting deadlines, finishing projects, and accomplishing your goals. You've tried different tactics and techniques for overcoming procrastination, all without much success. Sometimes, you've wondered whether others are right—maybe the problem is that you're lazy or that you don't have enough discipline. But deep down, you know that there *has* to be more to procrastination than just not trying hard enough.

Here's the truth: Procrastination isn't about laziness or self-control; it's far more complex than that. In fact, it's so complex that medical and psychological researchers have been studying the topic for more than 200 years. Research really picked up in the 1950s and has exploded over the past decade, leading to new breakthroughs in our understanding of how procrastination really works. We now know that you can't overcome procrastination through willpower alone and that focusing on just "getting stuff done" doesn't create sustainable change. Real psychological factors drive procrastination, and understanding them is key to overcoming them.

That's where this book comes in. Together, we'll dive deep into the psychology of procrastination. In part 1, we'll learn what procrastination is, how it works, and why it's so hard to stop. We'll also address how procrastination relates to common mental health issues like depression, ADHD, perfectionism, and imposter syndrome. In part 2, we'll learn how to apply that knowledge to make lasting change. We'll tackle specific issues like how to get motivated, follow through, and finish what you start utilizing psychology-based techniques that address the root causes of procrastination. Along the way, we'll increase our understanding of the brain so that you can work *with* it, rather than against it.

Since we're going on this journey together, I should introduce myself. I'm Dr. Hayden Finch, and I'm a licensed clinical psychologist. I use research-based strategies to help people master their mental health. My passion for psychology began during my time as an undergraduate at Duke University, where I studied psychology and neuroscience. There, I worked in a memory research laboratory and volunteered at a state psychiatric hospital. Ultimately, I earned my doctorate in psychology with research on how the mind works and how it affects our everyday lives.

Today, I put that knowledge into practice running a mental health clinic, where I help people overcome their greatest mental health hurdles. I've worked with hundreds of clients—people with diagnoses ranging from anxiety to psychosis, who are all struggling with issues that run the gamut from perfectionism to procrastination. You'll hear some of their stories in this book (though I have changed their names to protect their privacy). Their experiences have shown me that while procrastination is sometimes benign, it's often much more consequential; in extreme cases, it can lead to divorces, bankruptcies, and severe health problems. But it doesn't have to be that way. This book is your resource for finally making lasting change.

While this book contains the information you need to take control of your procrastination, in order to truly make a change, you'll need to commit to actually reading it. Procrastinators have a tendency to start books but not finish them, in part because they lose track of why they wanted to read them in the first place. But I know that you really want to create sustainable change, so let's set some good habits from the very beginning. To help yourself start overcoming procrastination right now, take a moment and write down three reasons you want to finish this book.

For real: Get out a piece of paper, write down your reasons, and use the list as your bookmark, or get a sticky note and post it where you'll see it every day.

But reading this book alone isn't enough—actually *taking action* is the most important part. You can do this.

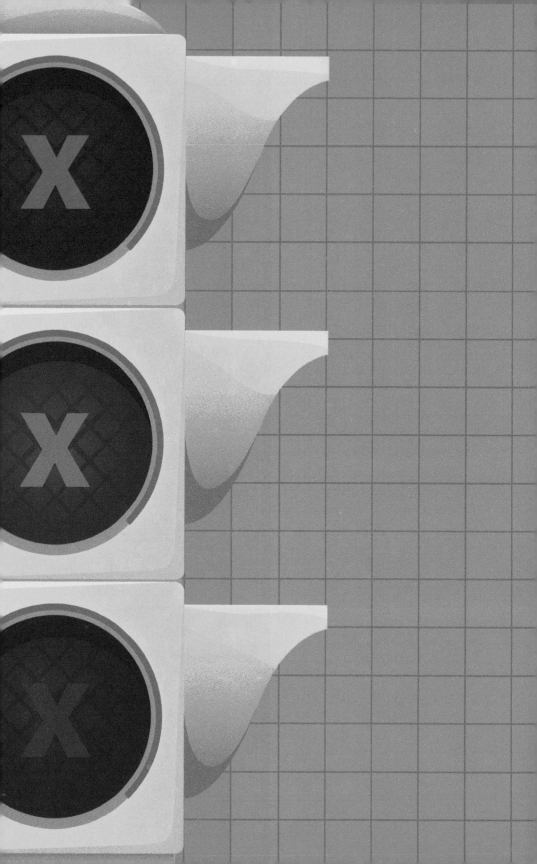

— — — — — — —

PART ONE

The Psychology of Procrastination

In part 1, we'll dive into the psychology of procrastination. We know full well that procrastination causes more problems than it solves, and we get frustrated with ourselves for continuing to procrastinate anyway. But we don't usually understand *why* we do it. In this section, you'll learn why we get stuck in that cycle, as well as all the psychological factors that cause us to repeat problematic behaviors. Plus, we'll look for some sneaky forms of procrastination that might be causing problems you don't even recognize yet. Then, we'll answer your most pressing procrastination questions, like *Why does procrastination happen? When does it become a problem? And whom does it affect the most?*

CHAPTER ONE

Understanding Procrastination

The first step in changing any behavior is to become aware of the behavior itself. Before we can stop and eventually reverse procrastination, we must be able to recognize it as soon as it starts. Procrastination can be sneaky—we might not notice when we procrastinate certain tasks, or we might procrastinate in ways that don't *look* like procrastination. That's why a thorough understanding of what procrastination is, what it looks like, and how it presents in life is so crucial. This knowledge helps us detect it early. And just like in medicine, early detection is the best prevention.

What Is Procrastination?

The word "procrastinate" comes from a combination of the Latin words *pro*, meaning "in favor of," and *crastinus,* meaning "of tomorrow." Broadly, procrastination means putting off a task or decision, even though you know you'll be worse off for delaying it. More specifically, it means putting off a task that you intend to do. At any given moment, you *could* be doing thousands of things; it's only procrastination when you're not tackling specific tasks or decisions that you've planned on accomplishing. So, not painting the house only counts as procrastination if you've been meaning to paint it; if you don't live in a house or your house doesn't need painting, then it's not procrastination.

In general, decisions and tasks that we consider valuable are less likely to be procrastinated than tasks we see as less valuable. For example, if you value personal style, you likely don't procrastinate shopping for new clothes; but if you find thriftiness to be more valuable, you might put off clothes shopping and rock your old JNCO jeans until they're threadbare. There's nothing inherently right or wrong about either approach. Our values help shape our decisions about the types of activities we postpone.

Procrastination can show up in nearly every area of your life. Though the most obvious form of procrastination might be putting off starting or finishing school and work assignments, procrastination extends beyond missing deadlines. We also put off making phone calls, completing paperwork, doing research or studying, and asking for help. Outside of work and school, we procrastinate on our daily chores, household maintenance, spring cleaning, buying groceries, or running errands. We also procrastinate financially, delaying things like paying bills, setting a budget, refinancing loans, paying off debts, and filing taxes. And we procrastinate socially, postponing making plans with our friends, calling our grandmas, and replying to RSVPs. We even procrastinate personally, never getting around to making therapy appointments, going to church, reading books, or developing hobbies. Health might be the sneakiest area of all: We put off making appointments for checkups, starting a healthier diet or exercise regimen, or quitting smoking or drinking. Anywhere there's an activity, task, behavior, or decision, there's room for procrastination.

Doing Something Against Your Better Judgment

Procrastination isn't just about delaying a task or decision—it's about delaying it without a good reason. Sometimes, we simply forget about something we should do. Other times, we'll put something off without considering how delaying it will affect us in the future. But often, we put things off despite *knowing* that it will cost us later—creating extra stress, lowering the quality of our work, or compromising our peace of mind. It's like when you have a free Saturday with literally *nothing to do*, and you spend it on a *Game of Thrones* binge instead of cleaning the house for your friend's upcoming visit. We've all done it. It's irrational, but much of human psychology is.

Procrastinators often know what they want to do or ought to be doing, have the *ability* to do it, and on some level, are *trying* to do it. But against their better judgement, they just don't do it. Between their initial intention to complete a task and actually setting out to do that task, they instead choose another course of action. This is why when you go to bed at night, getting up early to work out seems like a great idea, but between bedtime and waking up, your brain decides *not* working out is an even better idea.

Types of Procrastination

Not all procrastination is the same. We can sort the ways we procrastinate into two types: *passive* and *active* procrastination.

Passive procrastination is probably what you picture when you hear the word "procrastinate." This is when you mean to get started on something but just keep putting it off. If you find yourself repeatedly and honestly thinking, "I'll do it right after I finish this other thing," then you might be engaging in passive procrastination.

Passive procrastinators frequently avoid deadlines and decisions. Even *after* they've made decisions, they keep on avoiding and postponing taking action. They usually don't mean to procrastinate, but time has a way of getting away from them. The passive procrastinator plans to get that maybe-it's-a-freckle-maybe-it's-melanoma situation checked out but never gets around to making a doctor's appointment, or they keep meaning to call mom for her birthday that was three months ago.

Frequently, this type of procrastination is followed by guilt after it becomes clear that deadlines have passed or opportunities are gone. It's associated with a host of negative outcomes, ranging from lower psychological well-being to reduced personal growth and compromised relationships.

Active procrastination is much more deliberate. This is when you intentionally make a decision to procrastinate, often because you believe you "work better under pressure."

Active procrastinators make intentional, focused decisions to postpone activities and decisions, believing that the time pressure will enhance their abilities. This is you every time you try to convince yourself that you write your best papers when you're up against a deadline and then wait to get started until the 11th hour, when you're hyped up on caffeine, sleep deprivation, and panic.

Amazingly, sometimes these folks are right! They can rally their energy, creativity, and motivation to produce some stellar work at the last minute. But they also recognize that there have certainly been times when they came up short and fell victim to their own procrastination. Research tells us this type of procrastination usually isn't as detrimental as passive procrastination, but that's not to say that it's benign.

Everyone Procrastinates

Sorting people into groups of passive procrastinators and active procrastinators can disguise the fact that, in reality, everyone procrastinates at least a little. Most of us don't file our taxes on January 1st, schedule our dog's next grooming appointment while we're still at the salon, or scrub a mark off the wall the first time we see it. Since we have a finite amount of time and energy each day, everyone is forced to postpone some tasks.

But, as procrastination researcher Dr. Joseph Ferrari says, "Everyone procrastinates, but not everyone is a procrastinator." The difference between procrastinating and being a procrastinator is how habitual the procrastination is and how detrimental it becomes to your life. Ultimately, procrastination exists on a spectrum from "isolated, random instances" to "chronic and affecting just about everything in your life." We're all somewhere on that spectrum.

But I'm Doing Something: Procrastibaking, Detailed Lists, and Other Things That Feel Productive but Aren't

The tricky thing about recognizing procrastination is that when we're procrastinating, we're still doing other things. It's not like we decide to put something off and then just sit around and do nothing. We're masters at replacing one task with another task that's also important but maybe not quite as crucial. By doing this, we convince ourselves that maybe we aren't *actually* procrastinating—we're just busy!

Perhaps you've heard of procrasti*baking*, the practice of baking something unnecessary in order to put off doing something important? You can apply this to a wide array of activities—procrasti*plating* (that's when you procrastinate by cooking), procrasti*skating* (procrastination by skating), procrasti*baiting* (procrastination by fishing), procrasti*gaiting* (procrastination by running), procrasti*dating* (procrastination by dating), or even procrasti*mating* (you can guess that one!). We can procrastinate with essentially *any* task because the essence of procrastination is postponing one task and replacing it with something that's less important or more tempting.

By staying in motion, we convince ourselves that we're working toward a goal and that our procrastination really isn't all that bad. We can review how we spent the day, check things off a list, and feel accomplished. But when we challenge this idea, we see that we've procrastinated by prioritizing less important or urgent tasks or by fixating on unimportant details. So maybe you *did* get started on that massive work project, but instead of making a plan and then moving forward with it, you fixated on the plan and wrote a list, copied the list, color-coded the list, added items you've already completed to the list, splurged on ornamental paper to make the list extra special, rewrote the list in calligraphy, and posted an Instagram story showing off your fancy list. So, yes, you're working on that project—but you're doing more procrastinating than working.

When Does Procrastination Become a Problem?

We often use enjoyable activities to procrastinate, so procrastinating can feel really fun sometimes. But in reality, procrastination can have some pretty devastating consequences.

Talia, a brilliant and hard-working pre-med student, needed to take the MCAT, the medical school admissions test, so that she could apply to medical school in the fall. But she was afraid—her performance on that one test could determine her entire future. So instead of preparing for the MCAT, she procrastinated by studying for her classes and being active in school organizations. On the surface, this didn't look like procrastination *at all*. But she delayed registering to take the MCAT, which allowed her to delay studying for this essential exam. Ultimately, she postponed the decision for so long that there were no more seats to take the exam in the summer, which forced her to delay her entrance to medical school for an entire year. She felt ashamed as her peers began medical school the following year, while she was working at a bookstore and living with her parents.

Procrastination becomes problematic when it causes self-criticism and emotional distress—in Talia's case, it led to shame and thinking of herself as "stupid" for putting herself in that position. It's also problematic when it causes real-life detrimental outcomes, like Talia's missed opportunity to attend medical school with her peers. But procrastination doesn't have to ruin someone's life to be an issue; it's also problematic when it's habitual and leads to frequent smaller punishments, lost opportunities, or other issues that accumulate over time.

Chronic Procrastination

Even though 100 percent of us procrastinate with some things sometimes, 20 percent of us are chronically affected by procrastination (Harriott and Ferrari, 1996). The problem is even worse in college settings, where between 70 percent and 95 percent of university students consider themselves to be procrastinators and more than *half* report that it's a major problem (Steel, 2007). Not only are there many people who procrastinate, but it also takes up much of their time: Students admit to spending more than a third of their day procrastinating (Pychyl, Lee, Thibodeau, and Blunt, 2000). And more than 95 percent of procrastinators recognize that it's a harmful habit and want to overcome it (Briodi, 1980; O'Brien, 2002).

Research tells us that students don't procrastinate because they don't know how to study or get organized or because they're confused about how to manage their time. The same is true for adults in the working world, as well. People procrastinate due to a very complex interaction of psychological factors. These factors include the way our brains process information in our environment, past experiences we've had with procrastination and failure, the actions we take when procrastination is an option, and the thoughts and feelings we experience when we try to engage in difficult tasks. Plus, a tendency to procrastinate is inherited to some degree. All of this tells us that procrastination isn't an issue of laziness or effort; it's a psychological issue, which means we can use psychology to overcome it.

IS PROCRASTINATION A PROBLEM FOR ME?

If everyone procrastinates to some extent, how do you know if it's a real problem for you? Here are some questions, adapted from a number of well-known assessment questionnaires, to ask yourself.

1. Do you put off things you need to do, even when they're important?
2. Has putting things off until the last minute cost you money in the past (late payment fees, etc.)?
3. Do you tend to only make decisions when you're really forced to?
4. Do your friends and family get mad at you for not following through with what you say you're going to do?
5. Do you usually finish important jobs at the last minute?
6. Do you put things off for so long that you cause yourself unnecessary stress?
7. Do you put off quick, simple tasks for an unnecessarily long amount of time?
8. Do you experience problems because you run out of time to get things done?
9. When you've got a deadline approaching, do you waste time doing other things?
10. Would your life be better if you started some activities or tasks sooner?

If you answered "Yes" to more than four of these questions, you might have a problematic level of procrastination. But determining whether procrastination is a problem isn't as simple as analyzing how often you procrastinate or even identifying the types of activities or decisions you procrastinate. It's also about determining how much damage it's causing to your life. If you answered "Yes" to more than one of the even-numbered questions, you're recognizing that procrastination isn't just a habitual or frequent occurrence in your life—it's detrimental and is costing you money, relationships, opportunities, and your emotional well-being.

Psychology Can Help

People have been writing about problematic procrastination for more than 2,500 years, but until recently, we haven't really had much guidance regarding why it occurs or how to overcome it. Psychology is a relatively new field, and experimental research on procrastination only began in the 1980s; almost two-thirds of the research on procrastination has been conducted in the past decade. In that decade, psychologists have looked at how procrastination relates to personality traits and mental health conditions, developed questionnaires and instruments to measure it, investigated the associated brain areas, examined how other animals procrastinate, and asked questions like "Why in the world do people procrastinate going to sleep?"

For hundreds of years, humans mistakenly believed procrastination was a moral failing. Science has now proven that it's a complex and treatable psychological condition. Just about every person who walks into my clinic is struggling with procrastination in one form or another. Most of these clients postponed making their initial therapy appointment for months or years, and many of them continue to procrastinate in therapy—they delay telling me about important issues, and they definitely postpone doing their therapy homework. Procrastination is a symptom of just about every mental health condition. It's a symptom of depression, where folks delay getting out of bed or visiting friends, as well as a symptom of anxiety, where people delay making decisions until they can be guaranteed they're making the *right* decision. And in ADHD, procrastination is just rampant.

Over the next few chapters, we'll work together to understand the root causes of procrastination and begin to formulate a plan to overcome it. Let's start by digging deeper into the causes and effects of procrastination.

CHAPTER TWO

The Cycle of Procrastination

Now that you understand what procrastination is and how it shows up in your life, it's time to dive into why it's so hard to just stop doing it. When we procrastinate, we actually get stuck in a spiral, where one bout of procrastinating leads to another. One day of that turns into one week, which turns into one month, and before you know it, you've been procrastinating your life away for years. Understanding how that cycle works is a major step in extracting yourself from it.

Many Causes

Like any complex psychological phenomenon, procrastination is the end product of many factors. Deficits in skills like time management and assertiveness (e.g., overcommitting yourself) can contribute to procrastination, but they don't exactly *cause* it. Ultimately, it's a combination of the way your brain processes information, the feelings you have, how you estimate time, and the way you think. The more you understand about the factors causing your procrastination, the better equipped you'll be to start tackling it.

Self-Control and Motivation

When we talk about procrastination, we often phrase it like a motivational issue: "I'm just not motivated to work out today," "I don't feel like mopping the floor," or "I'm not feeling inspired enough to work on that paper right now." But procrastinators *do* feel motivation sometimes. It's just that their motivation to complete a task increases as the deadline approaches—a phenomenon called "hyperbolic discounting." This is partly caused by their tendency to focus on what's right in front of them, as well as their difficulty delaying gratification. Due to their preference for immediate rewards and pleasures, procrastinators usually start their day with the more pleasurable tasks, whereas non-procrastinators tend to prefer to get the hard stuff out of the way first.

Procrastinators also have trouble managing setbacks and tend to give up when they run into a problem. Lacking confidence that you can resist distractions or solve problems and accomplish your goals is a huge drag on self-control and motivation, and this is one factor that ultimately causes procrastination.

Procrastination is also influenced by our ability to monitor ourselves to see if we're on track with our goals. Every time you realize you ate an entire package of Oreos while you were still inside the grocery store, that's self-monitoring. And every time you realize you spent the last three hours playing video games instead of cleaning the house like you said you would, that's self-monitoring, too. You recognized that there was a difference between what you were intending to do and what you actually did. While we all have moments when we don't monitor ourselves well, procrastinators tend to struggle fairly routinely with this type of self-monitoring. Without self-monitoring, procrastination can hide in plain sight.

Difficulty Handling Negative Emotions

Procrastinators reliably choose to do more work later over less work now, partly because of the feelings associated with starting tasks—feelings like uncertainty, lethargy, or exasperation. When it comes to feelings, procrastinators are much more focused on how they're feeling *right now* than how they might feel later or even what their long-term goals are. Plus, they view tasks as much more aversive than most people would, which might be because they're more prone to boredom than non-procrastinators. The perception that tasks are aversive then creates even stronger negative emotions, which strengthens the impulse to procrastinate as a way of avoiding those feelings.

Sophia was a PhD student who needed to do a *lot* of writing to complete her dissertation. That type of writing creates considerable anxiety and stress, which she understandably wanted to avoid—by gardening. She's like anyone else in this way; the tasks most likely to be procrastinated are the ones that generate the most negative emotions and are boring, challenging, or tedious.

Sophia felt frustrated when she sat down to write and then relieved when she decided to put it off. Her brain realized that relief was better than anxiety and learned to encourage her to procrastinate every time she thought about writing. Like many other procrastinators, Sophia developed a habit of avoiding her feelings, and she did this so quickly and automatically that she hardly even noticed the feelings before her brain was already shutting them down.

You can't really blame Sophia for wanting to avoid her feelings about writing. Society has taught us that feelings are scary and we should avoid them. Feeling insecure when you have to go to a group event? Here, drink some cocktails and you won't notice your insecurity anymore. While we all want to avoid feeling uncomfortable feelings, procrastinators tend to feel uncomfortable feelings more strongly, are more impatient when tolerating discomfort, and have less practice coping effectively with discomfort. Those characteristics can perpetuate emotional avoidance and, ultimately, procrastination.

This strategy of coping with your feelings by avoiding them is a major contributing factor to procrastination.

You're Not Kind to Future You

Chances are high that you've never jumped out of an airplane. But even though you've never done it, your brain can imagine to some degree what it would be like to skydive. In fact, your brain's ability to forecast just how frightening it would feel to jump out of a plane is probably one of the things that's kept you from ever doing it.

This ability to simulate the future—which gives Present You a chance to walk in Future You's shoes—provides human brains with a huge evolutionary advantage, but it also has some limitations. For one, the simulations don't predict emotional intensity well. We imagine it's scary jumping out of a plane, but it's *definitely* scarier once a 200-pound man strapped to your back scoots your toes to the edge. Jumping out of the plane is just some abstract idea that's somewhat disconnected from reality until it's actually happening. In the same way, what Future You will be thinking and feeling is just an abstract idea until Future You becomes Present You.

When we make a decision to put something off, we can simulate what the consequences of that decision will be—we'll have less time to work on something, people might get frustrated with us, and we might run into unexpected problems. But the simulation of what our procrastination will feel like is usually more charitable than the reality—we underestimate the stress it will cause, the guilt we'll feel for continuing the pattern, or the disappointment that will stem from a missed opportunity.

So, even the best human simulators have limitations. Procrastinators' simulators are weak in general, and they struggle to consider the consequences of their choices. They're more concerned about what they're doing and how they're feeling in this moment and less concerned about the future. As a result, they keep prioritizing what they want right now over what they'll need in the future.

Unrealistic Ideas About Time

You know what else our brains are bad at? Estimating time. We don't have the slightest idea how long it takes us to do things. Even when Google tells you it takes exactly 23 minutes to drive to the airport, you still show up late because you forget to factor in the five minutes it takes to load up the car with your suitcases, the 12 minutes it takes to park the car and ride the shuttle to the airport, and the three minutes it takes to figure out how to get to the security line. Suddenly, your plan to show up early for your flight has turned into you rolling up to the gate just as boarding begins for your plane.

We also overestimate time. You might think scheduling three hours to get to the airport sounds right, and then find yourself sitting around for two entire hours, trying on perfumes in the duty-free shop. Almost all of us have experienced this. Humans are just not good at understanding time.

Both tendencies have consequences for procrastination. When we underestimate how long something will take us, we put it off, believing we'll have time to adequately complete the job later. This is why you consistently believe you can start cooking dinner 10 minutes before your guests start arriving.

When we overestimate how long something will take us, we think we don't have enough time to complete the task—so we put it off, waiting for another day when we'll magically have a bunch of extra time. This is why you avoid changing the sheets on your bed—though it actually only takes five minutes, you believe it's a 20-minute project that you just don't have time for right now. Overestimating how long something will take us can also make us feel overwhelmed. Then, we'll procrastinate because we want to avoid getting ourselves involved in a task that's intense. This brings us back to the way emotions keep procrastination going.

Waiting for "The Perfect Time"

When we overestimate how much time a task will require, we get into an especially sticky area of procrastination—waiting for the "perfect" time. The "perfect" time is when we're not tired, we feel inspired, there's nothing better going on, there's a motivating sense of urgency, and we have all the materials we need to complete the entire task.

Maybe the truth is that we *are* tired, we *don't* feel like doing it, there *are* more enjoyable activities to do, and we *don't* have enough time to complete the entire task today. But even if those things are true, it doesn't mean we can't get started. Most tasks can be broken down into parts, so even if you don't have the time to complete an entire project today, you could probably get *something* done now.

That "perfect" time is a unicorn. It doesn't really exist. For example, if your goal is to start working out at home to some cardio videos you found on YouTube, you'll never find the "perfect" time. The chance that you'll find a time when you're not tired, have nothing better to do, and actually *feel like* working out is zero. If you really want to accomplish this goal, you'll have to make it work at an inopportune time. We need to be honest with ourselves and acknowledge that the universe will never gift us space in our lives when we have nothing else to do.

Other Causes

Waiting for the "perfect" time isn't the only thought process that can under-mine your ability to take action.

One major cause of procrastination is a fear of failing, which sounds like, "If I start this new diet, I'll probably only do it for a couple of days before I mess it up," or "My résumé has to be perfect before I can apply for that job." Those kinds of thoughts easily prevent someone from starting a diet or applying for a job, period.

Related to a fear of failure is a fear of uncertainty, when we tell ourselves there must be a guaranteed good outcome before we can get started. This often sounds like, "Well, I don't really like my job, but if I tried to get another one, it might be even worse. Nothing bad can happen if nothing changes, so I'll just keep doing what I'm doing."

We also procrastinate by believing that our energy is too low to get started on something ("I'm too tired [or hungover, or anxious, or hormonal, etc.] to work on this.") or by getting lost in stubborn, rebellious thinking ("My way is better," or "I shouldn't have to do what other people tell me to do.")

And of course, there's everyone's favorite feeling, FOMO, or "fear of missing out." This comes with thoughts like, "Life's too short to be skipping out on fun things, just to complete some boring task."

Any of these thought processes can lead to procrastination because they turn into excuses, validating the decision to put something off.

Procrastination isn't always the product of a specific thought process, however. Sometimes, the way our brains parse information can make it difficult to get started on a task. Procrastinators tend to have a harder time recalling what tasks didn't get done yesterday, which means those tasks continue to go uncompleted. Plus, some procrastinators get distracted from tasks before they're completed, including decisions they're trying to make. This can result in indecisiveness or other forms of procrastination. And there's some evidence that when you're feeling negatively about a task (like working on that term paper), it gets harder for your brain to remember why that task is meaningful or personally valuable (like how much it will benefit your family for you to finish your degree). This makes it more likely that that task will be procrastinated.

Ultimately, procrastination isn't caused by one single factor. Instead, it's a combination of many things, including your genetics, the way your brain works, the types of thoughts and feelings you have, and the choices you make.

MYTHS ABOUT PROCRASTINATION

MYTH: PROCRASTINATION IS A TIME-MANAGEMENT PROBLEM.

- -

REALITY: Whether we're procrastinating or not, there are still 24 hours in a day and seven days in a week. Time can't really be managed, but activities and decisions can. Procrastination is less a time-management problem than an activity- or decision-management problem.

MYTH: PROCRASTINATORS WORK BEST UNDER PRESSURE.

- -

REALITY: Studies have shown that time pressure actually causes procrastinators to do a *worse* job on tasks. Under time pressure, they are slower and make more errors than non-procrastinators.

MYTH: TECHNOLOGY MAKES IT EASIER TO PROCRASTINATE.

- -

REALITY: Some of the activities we procrastinate *with* (e.g., video games) are new to the digital age, and the deadlines and commitments we have in industrialized societies make procrastination more obvious and problematic. But people have been procrastinating by reading, socializing, and doing nothing for thousands of years.

MYTH: NO ONE SUFFERS FROM MY PROCRASTINATION.

REALITY: Your coworkers suffer when you don't respond to emails in a timely manner, your partner suffers when you don't do your share of the chores, and your children suffer when you postpone taking care of your mental health and subject them to your stress and irritability. Because we're all connected, just about every instance of procrastination will affect someone who loves you, lives with you, or works with you.

MYTH: PEOPLE WHO PROCRASTINATE ARE LAZY.

REALITY: Procrastinators' brains are objectively different from the brains of non-procrastinators. These differences make it harder for them to motivate themselves, initiate tasks, delay temptation, and follow through with their intentions.

What Happens When You
Put Things Off?

Though you may believe that procrastination only has immediate ramifications—
that marked-down grade on your late term paper, the fee added to your
overdue credit card payment—it actually has long-term consequences that
touch almost every area of your life. Procrastinators have poorer health,
greater risk for mental health conditions, lower self-esteem, lower salaries,
shorter periods of employment, greater risk of unemployment, and general
misery. Let's look at some examples of what happens to your life when you put
things off.

Your Mental and Physical Health Decline

I met Ashley after her first semester of law school. She hadn't managed her
assignments well and by the end of the semester, she was depressed and discouraged about her ability to ever become an attorney. She was also having
panic attacks caused by severe stress.

Like Ashley, 94 percent of procrastinators report that procrastinating
has a negative impact on their happiness (Steel, 2007). When procrastination causes emotional distress, they tend to engage in fewer healthy coping
strategies to mitigate that distress, which means procrastination ultimately
contributes to self-blame, self-criticism, anxiety, depression, and per-
ceived stress.

Sometimes, we use procrastination as a way to reduce stress, thinking, "If
I postpone studying for the test, then I'll feel less stressed now." And that's
true—as long as the test is far away. But as the test date approaches, procrastinators actually feel even *more* stressed and have more physical health
problems (headaches, digestive issues, colds and flus, insomnia, etc.) than
non-procrastinators. It's not just that they're transferring the same amount
of stress to a later time point; research shows that they actually create *more*
stress for themselves overall by procrastinating.

Procrastination creates stress (not the other way around, by the way), and
stress then activates a host of physiological processes in your body. These
processes ultimately compromise your immunity and disrupt your body's
inflammatory processes. This increases your risk for health problems, including
high blood pressure and heart disease. Plus, that stress response discourages

us from doing the very things that keep us healthy, like exercising, eating healthy meals, and sleeping enough.

You Lose Money

Chronic procrastination doesn't just hurt your body and mind; it also hurts your wallet. A 2002 study by H&R Block (Kasper, 2004) found that 40 percent of Americans waited until April to file their taxes. Procrastinating on filing their taxes cost them $400 on average, due to late fees or errors caused by rushing through their work. The government got more than $473 million in overpayments from Americans in 2002 due to these errors.

That same survey also found that many Americans procrastinate on saving for the future. This means instead of spending your retirement playing shuffleboard, bringing back the Macarena on the dance floor, and sipping cocktails on a private beach in Mexico, you'll still be holding down your 9-to-5 because you didn't save up for retirement.

Procrastination can cost money in lots of other, smaller ways, like incurring late fees because you didn't pay your bills on time, getting stuck with a sweater that looked *way* better in the catalog because you didn't get around to returning it in time, or having to pay for car service to the airport because you didn't leave early enough to use public transportation.

You Don't Do Your Best Work

In addition to compromising our financial well-being, procrastinating means we just don't do our best work. My client Mason put off writing a letter to his boss explaining his team's frustrations with the company's new policies. In the end, he only had an hour to write the entire thing. Rushed, he forgot some of their key concerns, didn't have time to have his team approve the letter, and made typos, which compromised how seriously his boss took the team's complaints. Mason's story is relatable because procrastinators often produce inferior work. At school, this shows up as lower grades on assignments and exams, lower GPAs, and greater likelihood of withdrawing from courses. But even after graduation, procrastination is associated with compromised work quality.

Your Relationships Suffer

One of the most brilliant clients I ever worked with came to me because he had procrastinated so much that his marriage was falling apart. Michael, 42, was a highly successful business owner with a strong marriage, who would be anyone's nominee for "Dad of the Year." For years, he failed to keep track of his business's finances—it just never seemed urgent enough. But small book-keeping errors added up until the business was in serious jeopardy. That, of course, meant his family's welfare, security, and relationships were in jeopardy, as well. Without a profitable business, they couldn't afford their home, their Disney vacation, or even their five-year-old daughter's dance lessons.

Michael's story is one I hear often from my clients: They struggle so much to get motivated that their relationships fall apart. In fact, if I'm honest, the *relationship* piece is what gets people into my office more than anything else. We can pretend everything's fine until the people we love are impacted.

We think of procrastination as a *me* problem. Who cares if I stay up all night finishing a project or put off folding my clothes? It's not hurting anyone but me. But in many cases, procrastination is actually a *we* problem. Michael procrastinated paying bills and filing taxes, and his wife felt betrayed, deceived, and resentful as a result. She couldn't trust him with the business anymore, she couldn't depend on him to ask for help when needed, and she was constantly afraid he was hiding more. The long-term financial impact of his procrastination made her feel vulnerable, scared, and angry.

You don't have to be a parent or a business owner to have procrastination damage your relationships. When we don't respond to our coworkers' emails or phone calls in a timely manner, when we avoid discussing relationship prob-lems with our partners, and when we delay making plans with our friends, we create extra problems for the people around us. In short, we turn *me* procras-tination into *we* annoyance, exasperation, and irritation.

You Feel Good . . . Until You Don't

Procrastination causes some problems, but it also feels really good. It's so much more enjoyable to spend a night watching Netflix, scrolling Instagram, and clicking "Add to Cart" than it is to spend that time folding clothes, creat-ing a budget, and updating your résumé.

At least for a minute. But later on, of course, we have to pay for procras-tinating on important tasks. "Paying" for it can mean feeling stressed while we rush to get things done at the last minute, feeling demoralized by unmet goals, feeling defeated by mounting incomplete tasks, and feeling ashamed of how procrastination has affected the people we love. Ultimately, the guilt we feel for repeating the cycle and letting ourselves down (. . . again) taints the enjoyable activities we're procrastinating with.

A NEUROSCIENCE PERSPECTIVE

Procrastination is largely influenced by how certain parts of the brain work and how they communicate with each other (Zhang, Becker, Chen, and Feng, 2019; Zhang, Wang, and Feng, 2016). For example, procrastination is associated with more activity in the ventromedial prefrontal cortex, which helps us choose actions that are consistent with our values, and less activity in the anterior prefrontal cortex, which is involved in long-term planning. This combination means procrastinators tend to focus more on short-term, immediate satisfaction rather than long-term goals.

Procrastination is also influenced by how different areas of the brain interact with each other. For example, procrastination is associated with less interaction between the areas involved in making decisions. These disruptions interfere with our ability to choose broccoli over brownies or pick budgeting over procrastibaking.

Brain areas involved in the body's response to stress are also important in understanding procrastination. For example, stress activates the amygdala, which is involved in processing fear and other emotions. When the amygdala activates, it shifts our focus from the future to the present, so we can deal with an active threat. This is very useful when we're, say, being chased by a tiger. But when the stress is caused by procrastination, the amygdala activation means that we focus more on what feels good in the moment, even if this causes more problems down the road.

Why Procrastinators Don't Learn from Their Behavior and Experiences

We generally assume that procrastination is a problem of organization or time management. And it can be, in part. But as we discussed earlier, it's actually as much about feelings as it is about behaviors. When we think about a task we need to do, we start to feel some pretty uncomfortable feelings: overwhelmed, bored, immobilized, burdened, etc. Most humans don't like feelings, so we try to figure out a way to dodge or avoid them. Of course, procrastinating means we don't accomplish whatever task we were thinking about doing, but it also means that we save ourselves from feeling uncomfortable. The relief we feel from postponing a task and avoiding those feelings is addictive and makes us more likely to procrastinate the next time those same feelings pop up again. In other words, we're actually conditioning ourselves to continue to procrastinate.

Understanding the Cycle

Now that you know how procrastination works, let's look at how its components work together to keep us stuck in a cycle. When we think about doing a task, we start to have some predictable thoughts: "I don't have the energy right now," or "I'll do it later." We also start to have some pretty uncomfortable feelings—we might feel tense, discouraged, drained, or intimidated. We then have thoughts about those feelings: "Ugh, this sucks," "I can't stand this," or "I hate this feeling." A really strong desire to avoid those feelings develops. When we realize that we could get rid of those feelings by just *not* doing the task, we start working really hard to come up with some high-quality excuses to avoid the task. Instead of doing whatever task we should be doing, we choose something more pleasurable, or at least less overwhelming or distressing. Even though that creates some new problems, it also relieves those uncomfortable feelings we had just a second ago. That immediate relief is much more rewarding to us than the long-term benefits of not procrastinating, so our urge to procrastinate gets stronger. Plus, all the problems that accumulate while we're procrastinating (incomplete tasks, resentful family members) make us even more uncomfortable when we think about doing tasks, giving us more bad feelings that we want to ignore, further perpetuating the cycle.

In fact, it's not that procrastinators don't learn from their behavior and experiences. They *do* learn. It's just that what they're learning is that procrastinating relieves an uncomfortable feeling immediately, whereas *not* procrastinating feels uncomfortable for longer. Our brains love immediate gratification, so procrastination persists.

Now that you know where procrastination comes from, why it happens, and how it impacts your life, it's time to discover how procrastination impacts your mental health. Even if you haven't been diagnosed with a mental health condition, chances are high that procrastination is affecting and is affected by your emotional and behavioral health.

CHAPTER THREE

When Other Issues Are in the Mix

Procrastination doesn't just cause mental health problems; it is also *caused by* mental health problems. If you experience difficulties with your mental health, keep in mind that books (regardless of how science-based they are) are no substitute for individualized treatment. Always consult with a mental health provider about your specific needs. The purpose of this section is not to replace the treatment you'd receive from a clinician, but to enhance your understanding of how procrastination might be related to your emotional and behavioral experience.

ADHD

The mental health condition most commonly associated with procrastination is Attention-Deficit/Hyperactivity Disorder, a mental health condition characterized by trouble concentrating, impulsive behavior, or both. Folks with ADHD often make silly mistakes, get sidetracked easily, have trouble meeting deadlines or managing their time, and lose things frequently.

Consider my client Tim, who was so inattentive that he somehow earned a degree and then landed a job in a field that he had no interest in. The problems inattention and distractibility created in his life were numerous—from unpaid bills, to physical injuries, to a disgruntled wife. That disgruntled wife is what ultimately led him to me. She would give him a list of tasks to complete on his day off, but he'd spend most of the day playing video games and then rush to complete the list just before she got home from work. He often didn't finish the list, and when she got home . . . well, you know how that story ends.

After experiencing so many versions of the same issue, Tim, like many people with ADHD, started to think there was something wrong with him, that he was incapable of getting his life together. These beliefs echoed in his head whenever he felt stressed, which made him feel depressed and anxious, which perpetuated his procrastination. But his wife was also impacted—she had to do more than her fair share of work around the house because Tim either delayed starting, left a task incomplete, or was unreliable.

Procrastination with ADHD can take many forms. Sometimes, it looks like Tim's life, where susceptibility to temptation and distraction prevents someone from effectively structuring their time. But it can also look like forgetfulness, trouble completing long-term projects, problems with organization or decision-making, or a tendency to avoid starting or finishing difficult, unpleasant, and uninteresting tasks.

ADHD procrastination stems from a different set of causes than procrastination related to other mental health conditions. For example, someone with depression might have trouble starting or finishing tasks because they lack energy, whereas someone with ADHD struggles with starting because of distractibility and difficulty delaying gratification. Someone with anxiety might avoid tasks because they're afraid of failure or uncertainty, but someone with ADHD more often avoids tasks because the tasks themselves are boring or tedious. However, it's common for a person with ADHD to also have depression and anxiety, meaning their procrastination can be the product of many different factors.

Tackling ADHD-Related Procrastination

There's considerable overlap in the brain areas affected by ADHD and procrastination. Just about every element of completing a task—including choosing the task, finding motivation to start, staying focused, following through, and finishing the task—can be challenging for someone with ADHD. But the primary factor affecting procrastination in ADHD is distractibility. As you read through part 2, consider concentrating on chapter 8 (see page 87) for strategies for getting focused and chapter 10 (see page 107) to learn how to finish what you've started. Finally, people with ADHD have particular difficulty organizing themselves, their tasks, and their time, so chapter 5 (see page 59), which focuses on how to establish priorities, may also be especially helpful.

Depression

A person experiencing depression usually feels sad, empty, irritable, or hopeless. Depression also changes sleep and appetite patterns. Like any mental health condition, depression exists on a spectrum: On one end are people who only occasionally feel blue and are still able to keep up with most of their normal activities; on the other are people who are chronically depressed and have trouble getting out of bed. Episodes of depression can occur repeatedly throughout a person's life, sometimes without any trigger or provocation; they can also occur just once, in response to a major adverse life event (like the death of a loved one).

When Nathan first called me, he admitted he'd been putting off starting therapy for years. But procrastination hadn't just kept him from making a therapy appointment: He'd also procrastinated on building relationships, finding an intellectually stimulating job, and getting involved in meaningful activities. Reflecting on his life, he believed he had little to live for and was seriously contemplating suicide. If you're thinking this relationship between procrastination and suicide is extreme, it's not. Procrastination is actually a major predictor of suicidal thoughts (especially in college-age women who have a low sense of self-worth).

Nathan had obviously put off the big things in life, but he was also procrastinating on all the little things, like tidying up his apartment, getting a haircut, and going to the grocery store. He put off work assignments until the very last minute, making his resentful teammates responsible for all other projects while he was rushing. He was eventually fired from his job. His family and friends were also impacted by his procrastination—he canceled plans and broke promises in order to get work projects done at the last minute, and his chronic tardiness made them late, too. But most important, they were in serious risk of losing him to suicide.

Procrastination stemming from depression has many similarities to procrastination associated with ADHD and anxiety; the primary difference is that a person with depression procrastinates because they lack the energy to start a task. Because someone with depression may also experience low self-esteem, perfectionism, or imposter syndrome, they may be dealing with several different types of procrastination.

Tackling Depression-Related Procrastination

Tackling depression-related procrastination can require special expertise. If you're struggling in this area, I strongly recommend that you also consult with a therapist or psychologist, who can help you address the root of your depression.

The low energy associated with depression makes it harder to get started with and complete tasks, so it may be helpful to focus your energy in that area. As you read part 2, try focusing on chapters 6, 7, and 9. In chapter 6 (see page 69), you'll learn strategies for finding motivation, which is helpful for overcoming the fatalistic pessimism we experience when we're depressed—those thoughts like "Why should I even bother to take a shower? No one's gonna smell me today." In chapter 7 (see page 79), you'll learn techniques for getting started with tasks. Those tips will help you overcome the hurdle of doing *something* when you really feel like doing *nothing*. And chapter 9 (see page 97) is all about overcoming avoidance. One lesser-known symptom of depression is indecisiveness; because everything feels really crappy when you're depressed, it's hard to make decisions about anything. We'll explore some strategies for making decisions so you can move forward with what is important to you.

Anxiety and Anxiety-Related Issues

Anxiety involves feelings of fearfulness, apprehensiveness, or uneasiness. This can include generalized anxiety, where someone worries about lots of different things (safety, money, job performance, physical appearance, or relationships); social anxiety, where someone fears being judged, scrutinized, or embarrassed; and OCD, where someone has intrusive thoughts about something bad happening and tries to get rid of those thoughts with compulsive behaviors.

There's a certain level of "normal" anxiety that everyone experiences to some degree. Just about everyone feels nervous stepping into a busy street without checking traffic first; if you didn't have that anxiety, you'd probably get hurt. Most of us feel anxious when giving a presentation; if you didn't have that anxiety, you might not take the presentation seriously and could disappoint your coworkers and lose your job. Anxiety is essential to survival, but some people have anxiety that seriously affects their quality of life. As with any other mental health condition, anxiety can range from mild and transient to severe and persistent.

Richard had a more chronic form of anxiety. He had fairly serious OCD—he doubted nearly everything he ever did or thought, and he coped with this by avoiding most tasks, like throwing away plastic bottles (maybe he'd need them one day) or checking the mail (what if he received some bad news?). One day, after grocery shopping, Richard forgot a gallon of milk he'd left in his car trunk. By the time he realized what had happened, the milk was spoiled, and he felt guilty for making this mistake. But instead of throwing the carton away, he avoided it. By avoiding it, he could avoid the guilt he felt about his mistake. But his guilt grew while the spoiled milk baked in the summer heat, eventually giving off a truly foul odor.

The milk example is extreme, but Richard's anxiety made him avoid far more than the gallon of milk. He avoided taking his medicine, brushing his teeth, and getting the heat in his apartment fixed. He felt overwhelmed by these tasks, pushed them off to relieve that feeling, and then felt guilty for delaying them. He was overcome with a fear of not doing tasks correctly, which kept him from even attempting them. His avoidance affected other people, too. Because he avoided saving money, he relied on credit cards, which created debt, lowered his credit score, and cost his family extra fees. All this, plus his tendency to avoid important conversations, meant his relationships slowly deteriorated.

As with depression and ADHD, it can be hard to get started on tasks when you're anxious, but this is most often due to feelings of being overwhelmed or worries about failing. As with ADHD, it can be hard to stay focused on a task, but with anxiety, this is more about being distracted by worries than being distracted by other temptations. An interesting component of anxiety-related procrastination is fear of finishing tasks successfully. Sometimes, people with anxiety are actually afraid of success: If I succeed, people might expect even more from me, and what if I can't meet their expectations? Better to put it off and just stay in this comfort zone of mediocrity, they decide.

Tackling Anxiety-Related Procrastination

The connection between anxiety and procrastination is largely related to feelings of being overwhelmed and fear—fear of success and fear of making mistakes. These fears make it harder to start and complete tasks and make decisions. If you can relate, consider focusing especially on chapters 7, 9, and 11. In chapter 7 (see page 79), you'll discover strategies for conquering overwhelmed feelings so you can get started on your task list. Then, in chapter 9 (see page 97), we'll work on indecisiveness and avoidance. People with anxiety often worry about making the "right" choice, and a fear of making the wrong choice can lead them to avoid decisions altogether. We'll look at some tips for managing avoidance and moving forward. And in chapter 11 (see page 115), we'll focus on how to finish what you started, even if you're afraid of what success could mean for you. Of course, a book is not a substitute for individualized mental health treatment—use these strategies in conjunction with a therapist or psychologist to ensure you're addressing your anxiety-related procrastination in the healthiest way for you.

PROCRASTINATION AND ADDICTION

When it comes to drugs and alcohol, procrastination has been linked strongly to marijuana use. Fifty-three percent of occasional marijuana users report that it causes them to procrastinate, but 94 percent of people who are dependent on marijuana report that it has led them to procrastinate. Likewise, procrastination has also been linked to using stimulants (like cocaine, speed, or Adderall) and intravenous drugs (like heroin), as well as to internet and social media addiction.

Procrastination isn't just a consequence of addiction; it can also be part of the cause. Research consistently shows that procrastinators get worried or anxious just before deadlines, and using drugs or engaging in other addictive activities can help relieve those feelings.

Plus, procrastination is part of what keeps people stuck in the addiction cycle. Researchers have called the repeated promise that tomorrow will be the day we stop drinking or smoking the "procrastination defense" (Clancy, 1961).

Self-Esteem and Self-Confidence

We sometimes use the terms "self-esteem" and "self-confidence" interchangeably, but they're actually very different, at least in psychology. Self-esteem refers to whether you have a positive or a negative attitude about yourself and think of yourself as good or bad. People with high self-esteem respect themselves and feel worthy, while acknowledging that they're not perfect;

people with low self-esteem can only see their weaknesses and feel unworthy or inadequate.

Caleb was exceptionally generous and loving; however, his low self-esteem made him think he was a terrible person. Caleb's low self-esteem kept him from asking for help when he needed it. He was nearly evicted from his apartment because he avoided asking for help when he was in serious financial trouble. Unfortunately, by trying to avoid causing problems for the people he loved, he sometimes created extra problems. For example, Caleb never wanted to upset his partner. So, to make sure they never had any serious, potentially upsetting conversations, he avoided spending much time with her. But by doing this, he put off improving their relationship.

While self-esteem is about how you evaluate yourself, self-confidence is about your belief that you can do something well. Michelle had been putting off her weight-loss goal for years. She wasn't confident she could make a suitable nutrition plan, follow through with exercising regularly, or lose the 150 pounds she needed to in order to be healthy. So, she put it off and continued to gain weight.

Procrastination stemming from low self-esteem and self-confidence limits the opportunities we pursue. We stay in unhealthy relationships too long, don't go after promotions, and don't pursue opportunities for personal growth. The people around us suffer, too: They don't get to see us thrive, and sometimes, they have to step in to do the things we're not confident enough to do for ourselves. We start to lead very small lives, thinking that's all we deserve or are capable of.

Procrastination stemming from low self-esteem or self-confidence often involves difficulty starting or finishing tasks, just like procrastination coming from ADHD, depression, or anxiety. But this form of procrastination stems from the belief that we don't deserve to get started or to find success, or that we're not capable of completing the tasks.

Tackling Esteem- and Confidence-Related Procrastination

Because the connection between self-esteem, self-confidence, and procrastination is largely related to what we think we deserve and are capable of, tackling this type of procrastination involves overcoming those unhelpful beliefs. As with any mental health condition, it's best to check in with a therapist or psychologist to provide tailored individual treatment if you're struggling with self-esteem or self-confidence. In addition, consider focusing on chapters 7, 10, and 11 of this book. The strategies in chapter 7 (see page 79) are designed to help you get over the barriers to getting started, even if you're feeling unsure about your ability to get to the end. When you hit a stumbling block, low self-confidence can make it hard to push through, so chapter 10 (see page 107) helps you resolve those setbacks and get back on track. When you've completed most of a task and are nearing the end, thoughts about whether you deserve success or can tackle what comes next can keep you from following through. The strategies in chapter 11 (see page 115) can help you finish what you started.

Perfectionism

Perfectionism involves setting exceptionally high standards for yourself and then tying your worth to your ability to meet those unreasonable standards. In some ways, this can be positive: Having high expectations for yourself can increase self-confidence and is actually associated with *less* procrastination. But perfectionism can also be detrimental: Criticizing yourself, worrying excessively about mistakes, and being unable to feel satisfaction even when you do a good job can cause anxiety and depression and increase procrastination.

Many of my clients are perfectionists, like Chloe, a meticulous CPA. The success she had built for herself was addictive. When she was young, she excelled in school and made the honor roll. Soon, she became terrified by the idea of not making the honor roll—who would she be then? Eventually, she developed a habit of procrastinating on her assignments and staying up all night to finish them right before they were due. As deadlines loomed, she'd spend hours obsessing over font choices, sentence structure, and formatting, making everything absolutely perfect. She realized delaying getting started was risky, but this way, if she didn't do well, it was because she didn't have enough time, not that she wasn't smart enough. In other words, to a perfectionist, procrastinating and failing is better than trying really hard and failing.

Perfectionists are often highly capable, but their unreasonable standards encourage them to put things off—and putting things off sabotages their ability to meet their own standards. The procrastination causes self-criticism (e.g., "I should have started sooner," or "I always mess this up"), and perfectionists often unintentionally transfer their pressure-driven intensity to the people around them, who believe they'll be criticized if they can't meet the perfectionist's standards. That's certainly what Chloe's husband felt; he thought he couldn't do anything right by her standards. Plus, because Chloe was so busy working on tasks she procrastinated due to perfectionism, her friends and family often missed out on time with her. She missed happy hours and her son's tee-ball games, and she frequently rescheduled dates with her husband, all to stay late at work.

As with anxiety, low self-esteem, and low self-confidence, perfectionists often procrastinate due to a fear of completing tasks and a preference to avoid feeling inadequate or afraid. Perfectionists don't feel satisfied after they succeed with a goal or task; instead, after a brief moment of relief, they reason that they should have set the bar even higher. Leaving a task unfinished can prevent a perfectionist from having to raise a standard that was already exceptionally high even higher.

Tackling Perfectionism-Related Procrastination

Some perfectionists have trouble getting started with tasks. This is motivated by a fear of failure—they think, "If I don't get started on a task, then I can't mess it up." But when it comes to perfectionism-related procrastination, the primary issue is completing tasks. Perfectionists put off finishing tasks as they strive to meet their own impossibly high standards. You can find tips on following through and finishing tasks you start in chapter 10 (see page 107) and chapter 11 (see page 115). When perfectionistic standards encourage you to give up, convince you you're not good enough, and make you fearful of failing (or even succeeding), these strategies will help you push through and overcome those barriers. And if you're one of the perfectionists who has trouble getting started with tasks, consider spending some time in chapter 7 (see page 79) to resolve the task-initiation barrier. As always, work in conjunction with a therapist or psychologist to make sure you're really addressing the root cause of your perfectionism and using the strategies that are the best for you.

Imposter Syndrome

Even if you've never heard of imposter syndrome, chances are high that you've experienced it. It's a fear of being exposed as an incompetent fraud, even when you're objectively competent. It's that feeling you get when you worry that you don't deserve a promotion you've clearly earned. That's exactly what happened to Christina. Even though she was qualified for a promotion, she feared she'd only deceived her supervisors into thinking she knew what she was doing. She was afraid she'd eventually be outed as a fraud.

Because she didn't feel worthy or capable of the promotion, Christina delayed applying for it for years. Those kinds of missed occupational and academic opportunities are some of the most common outcomes of imposter syndrome–related procrastination. People with imposter syndrome have trouble recognizing their own potential and don't pursue prestigious career opportunities they're likely qualified for. This holds them back professionally and financially.

But Christina wasn't the only one who was suffering due to her procrastination. Her reluctance to push herself at work meant she busied herself with relatively easy assignments, while her coworkers got stuck with the harder or more time-consuming tasks. And while prioritizing busyness helped her conceal feelings of inadequacy, it meant she wasn't available to work on her relationship or spend time with her children.

Because people with imposter syndrome doubt their capabilities and assume other people doubt them as well, their procrastination issues are similar to those of people with self-confidence issues. People with imposter syndrome are so focused on their inadequacies, flaws, and mistakes that they lean toward perfectionism to correct them, so perfectionism-related procrastination can show up, too.

Tackling Imposter Syndrome–Related Procrastination

The greatest barrier to overcoming imposter syndrome–related procrastination is getting started on tasks. Low self-confidence or low self-esteem makes us buy into the narrative that we aren't qualified enough to go after our goals. We'll delay applying for a new job, starting our own company, or writing a book. Or we'll get started during a rare burst of confidence but then talk ourselves out of completing these tasks. If you can relate, focus on chapter 7 (see page 79) and chapter 11 (see page 115), where you'll find strategies for getting started on your projects and finishing them, even if you're feeling like a total fraud. And, of course, make sure you're doing this in conjunction with a therapist who can help you get an individualized approach that addresses the root of your imposter syndrome.

What If It's Not Just One Thing?

Let's be honest: You can probably relate to more than one of the issues we covered in this chapter. Mental health conditions have a tendency to overlap, and many of them cause similar symptoms and problems. Your procrastination may stem from multiple issues. Maybe you put off cleaning your oven because of perfectionism, and then put off getting involved in a spiritual group because of self-esteem, and then put off opening your mail just because. You might have a few different areas to focus on, and that's normal. The quiz in chapter 4 (see page 46) will help you narrow your focus, so you'll have a plan for directing your energy.

And don't worry if the examples I provided didn't sound 100 percent like your experience. Procrastination, depression, anxiety, and other mental health conditions and issues really are individual—everyone feels them and expresses them differently. But the strategies you'll discover in part 2 have been proven to help people with all different kinds of experiences overcome procrastination. Rest assured that even if your version of procrastination feels a little bit different from the stories I've told here, the tips and strategies in part 2 will still help you.

Now you understand the psychology of procrastination—what causes it, when it becomes a problem, why it's such a hard cycle to stop, and the issues it can cause in your life. It's time to use that knowledge to start tackling the problem, which is exactly where we're headed in part 2. You're halfway done with this book, and the hard part (actually overcoming your procrastination) is coming up. Before we launch into it, go back to the note you made at the beginning of the book to remind yourself why you started reading it in the first place. Then, let's get our hands dirty and start overcoming your procrastination.

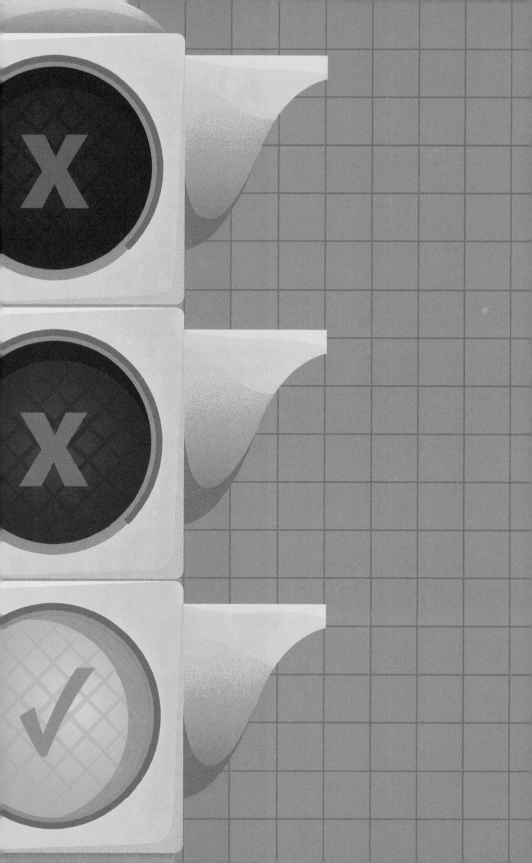

PART TWO

Using Psychology to Overcome Procrastination

In part 1, we covered the psychology of procrastination and discovered why it's so easy to get stuck in the cycle. Now it's time to use what you've learned to start breaking free from negative patterns that keep you from accomplishing your personal and professional goals. Part 2 starts with an overview of some general things to keep in mind as you start to tackle your procrastination. This will help you shift into a mindset to make changes. The rest of part 2 is loaded with specific, evidence-based tips and strategies to help you stop the procrastination cycle and start building some better habits. We'll work through strategies for each part of the procrastination cycle: from getting motivated to staying on task and finishing what you started. By the end, you'll have all the best tools psychological science has to offer, and you can use them to finally find freedom from your procrastination.

CHAPTER FOUR

Overcoming Procrastination

In part 1, you discovered how procrastination works, and now you're ready to tackle it in your own life. Before we dive into specific tips, though, it's important to review some general approaches to overcoming procrastination. It's like gardening: Before you start planting, you need to collect your seeds and dirt, monitor the sunlight and rain availability, and identify how far apart your plants need to be spaced— it's as much about the preparation as it is the actual work. Before you start using specific strategies to overcome pro- crastination, you need to keep some general concepts in mind so you can use the strategies more effectively.

Why You Procrastinate

In chapter 2, you learned what causes procrastination, and in the next few chapters, you'll start drilling down into your own unique root causes. Whether your procrastination comes from a mental health condition or just exists all on its own, it is caused by a combination of psychological factors, including how your brain works and how you think, feel, and behave, as well as how well you estimate time and whether you're able to focus on the future. But

WHAT TO WORK ON FIRST

You might struggle with every part of procrastination, from setting priorities to getting started to following through. That might make the very thought of trying to overcome procrastination feel overwhelming: Where do I even start? You might benefit from strategies in several (or even all!) of the following chapters, but let's focus on where you should start. Ask yourself:

1. When you make a to-do list, is it hard to know what to do first?
2. When you commit to doing something, do you sometimes forget why it's important to you?
3. Is it hard for you to get motivated to do boring, tedious, or unpleasant tasks?
4. Once you've decided to do a task, do you find that you usually don't know where to start?
5. Is it hard for you to get over the hump of getting started with a task?
6. Do you find it hard to concentrate on tasks?
7. Do you notice yourself feeling overwhelmed or anxious when you try to start working on tasks?
8. Is it hard for you to make decisions?

procrastination is primarily caused by the way you manage your feelings. Are you someone who's prone to boredom and needs excitement? Are you trying to avoid feeling inadequate or uncertain? Do you feel overwhelmed when you think about tasks? The feelings that come up when you think about doing a task, and the relief you experience when you put it off, are major clues about why *you* procrastinate.

9. Once you start tasks or projects, do you have trouble following through and completing them?
10. Does being afraid of making mistakes, failing, or even succeeding hold you back from completing what you've started?

If you answered "Yes" to:

Question 1, focus on chapter 5 first.

Questions 2 and 3, focus on chapter 6 first.

Questions 4 and 5, focus on chapter 7 first.

Question 6, focus on chapter 8 first.

Questions 7 or 8, focus on chapter 9 first.

Question 9, focus on chapter 10 first.

Question 10, focus on chapter 11 first.

If you answered "Yes" to several questions, start with chapter 5 and go in order.

The Truth About Conquering Procrastination

Time for a truth bomb: The strategies in this book aren't a quick fix. Not because they aren't good, but because there's no such thing as an actual quick fix. Yes, some self-help books promise you instant change, but I'd rather be honest than mislead you. Our brains are capable of changing—new pathways are built all the time, and sometimes new neurons grow—but these changes don't happen overnight. Our brains really want to make sure a new habit is useful before they abandon old ones; otherwise, it'd be a total waste of energy. If you've ever heard it takes 21 days, 30 days, or some other arbitrary number of days to change a habit, let me set you straight—that's not really what the science says. According to current research, it takes somewhere between 18 and 254 days to make a new habit, with about 66 days being the average (Lally, van Jaarsveld, Potts, and Wardle, 2010). And that's not 66 days of winging it; that's 66 days of strong, consistent, daily effort. So, if you're serious about overcoming procrastination, prepare yourself to try new strategies and conquer setbacks (and probably struggle, feel frustrated, and question why you even started) for *at least* a couple months, and possibly longer. None of this is to say that you can't change. It's totally possible to overcome procrastination. But it's best to know at the start that this will be a real commitment.

Telling Someone (or Yourself) to "Just Do It" Doesn't Help

I know you've tried the "just do it" strategy. You know, when you promise yourself that you're going to start going to the gym every morning but never seem to make it in before work—so you decide that you'll just have to *force* yourself to go. But, somehow, that doesn't work, either.

The issue is that the "just do it" approach doesn't address the root causes of procrastination; in fact, it completely ignores everything about the emotional sources of the problem. It doesn't give you any strategies for dealing with the emotions that come up when you think about going to the gym: the shame about being out of shape, the uncertainty about what to do once you're at the gym, the overwhelmed feeling when you think about how much work is needed to reach your fitness goals. Once those feelings bubble up, you're at a loss for how to manage them, and so you just do what you've always done: roll over and go back to sleep. Instead of ignoring those issues and telling yourself to "just do it," you need some actual evidence-based strategies to *solve* the issues that make you want to avoid those tasks. And that's where the strategies in chapters 5 through 11 come in.

It's Not Just About Time Management

Another misguided strategy is focusing exclusively on time management. Many people believe procrastination comes from poor organizational and time-management skills—like if we just had a better schedule and were more organized with our time, then we wouldn't procrastinate so much.

But here's how we know it's not that simple. William had some fairly straightforward but important goals he wanted to accomplish in therapy, one of which was to submit paperwork to reduce his student loan payments. Imagine (or maybe you don't have to imagine) having a student loan the size of your mortgage. That's the situation William was in. Every session, we'd meticulously schedule each step and troubleshoot any problems that could potentially ruin the plan. And yet, he didn't follow the plan. The problem clearly wasn't organization or time management—we addressed those issues. It became clear that, just like with getting to the gym, the problem was *feelings*. Something as major as a massive student loan payment carries a *lot* of intense feelings with it, and it made William feel helpless, intimidated, trapped, bitter, and burdened. Each time William set out to follow the plan we had so methodically crafted, these feelings cropped up again. He then had a choice: Keep following the plan and feel those awful feelings, or feel better by telling himself he'll just follow up with the loan company tomorrow. Guess which one he chose? Poor time management can certainly affect procrastination, and improving those skills can be helpful. But ultimately, overcoming procrastination requires addressing the deeper emotional causes.

Evidence-Based Strategies Help

Sometimes, people balk at psychology, saying it's a "common sense" science because some of the findings support what's obvious: Students who study more earn higher grades, using drugs damages your brain, and petting animals feels good. But often, the findings are surprising, or even the opposite of what you'd think: Screaming into a pillow when you're mad actually *worsens* anger, our memories include many errors, and opposites don't actually attract in relationships. That's why consulting the research is so important when you're overcoming any sort of psychological issue, including procrastination. Going with intuitive strategies can be helpful in some cases, but if you're looking for long-term, sustainable change, it's critical to choose approaches proven to address the psychological causes of the issue. Sometimes, these evidence-based strategies are intuitive and fit our common sense, and other times, they're the exact opposite of what you'd think to do. Good thing we have science to offer us guidance.

Focus on the Root Cause

To fix most problems, you have to start at the root. If your eyes are watering, for instance, it's helpful to know if that's being caused by seasonal allergies, an infection, or getting a bit of hot pepper in your eye. Then you know whether you should address the problem by taking an antihistamine, seeing a doctor, or remembering not to touch your eyes while you cook chili. The same is true with procrastination. When we address what's actually causing the procrastination, we're more likely to figure out an approach to treating it that will actually work. When we skip this step and just start trying to tackle procrastination all willy-nilly, it's like trying to treat pink eye with an antihistamine—it's just not very helpful.

By the way, determining the "root cause" of your procrastination doesn't mean going all the way back to the childhood moment that started you on this pathway. It just means isolating the thoughts, the behaviors, and especially the feelings that are keeping your procrastination alive. Once you know whether your procrastination is driven by problems with self-control or motivation, intolerance of feeling uncomfortable, unrealistic ideas about time, or any of the other causes we've addressed, you can determine the type of approach you need to overcome it. Then, chapters 5 through 11 will give you the right psychological strategies you need to tackle the problem.

Keep These Things in Mind

Though you'll need to utilize specific strategies to tackle your own procrastination, establishing a strong foundation of basics first can make these individual strategies more effective. It's kind of like how having a foundation of agility, fitness, and strength makes it easier to learn to play any sport, from soccer to basketball. So, regardless of what's causing your procrastination or which parts of completing a task are a struggle for you, the following considerations are applicable to everyone.

Practice Self-Compassion

As you try to overcome procrastination, you're destined to make mistakes. There will be times when you slide back into old habits, there will be strategies you just can't figure out how to implement, and there will be days when it just feels too overwhelming to keep working at it. Some people believe that, in these situations, criticizing themselves will prevent mistakes or provide motivation to get things done. If you are one of those people, ask yourself this: Has criticizing yourself in the past actually helped you get more done? Or did success come only after you developed and committed to a plan?

If you're a manager at work, you probably use kind, compassionate language when you're trying to motivate your employees. The same is true with children: When your child makes a mistake, I'll bet you try to kindly encourage her to change her behavior, rather than berate her for messing up. There's a reason we use kind, compassionate language to motivate others—it's simply more effective than criticism. Take the same approach with your own self-talk. When you criticize yourself for not having started, not having finished, or not working quickly enough, imagine what you would say to a friend, a child, or even your dog if they were having the same issue. Remember, we can't change what's already happened. So rather than focusing on what you already didn't do, try to focus instead on what you can do from here.

Work on Self-Awareness

Once you've changed the way you talk to yourself, it's important to start building self-awareness. Most of our behaviors are so automatic and habitual that we aren't even aware of them. We don't notice when we scratch our noses, and sometimes, we've driven halfway to work before we realize we have no memory of the last five miles. Lack of awareness isn't necessarily a problem when it comes to itchy noses or morning commutes, but it is when you're trying to change your behavior. If you're not aware something's happening, you can't change it.

Self-awareness is crucial because procrastination happens so quickly, it doesn't even feel like you made a choice to put something off; it's like it just magically happened. But it's not magic. In just a fraction of a second, you went through the entire process of thinking about doing something, feeling uncomfortable about doing it, and deciding to do something else so you could get rid of that discomfort.

Building self-awareness is challenging, so be patient with yourself and practice self-compassion. The best way to develop greater self-awareness is to choose an activity you do throughout the day and try to catch yourself doing it. Maybe it's sitting down, standing up, touching doorknobs, or taking a drink of water. Paying attention to those benign behaviors will train your brain to notice other things you're doing. Then, with some practice, you'll be able to catch yourself choosing to put off a task or getting sidetracked while you're working on something.

WHEN MEMORY IS AN ISSUE

Memory is a very complicated phenomenon. We each have several different types of memory—like memory for facts about the world (called semantic memory), memory for behaviors (procedural memory), and memory for life events (episodic or autobiographical memory), among others. The nature of memory also changes as we age. We have almost no memories of life events before age five, but we remember how to do tons of things we learned before age five, like how to walk and talk and how the world works. Certain memories will start to disappear with age, while others stick around forever.

Memory is also complicated because everyone's memory is different. Individual people vary in terms of how well they convert information into memories, how many memories they can store, and how long the memories stay in storage.

Because memory is so unique and individual, you know better than anyone else if you can rely on your own memory to remember tasks. If forgetfulness is contributing to your procrastination, it's helpful to use lists, reminders, calendars, and alarms to compensate for lapses in memory. Many people make lists and then forget to look at them, so take advantage of technology to remind yourself of important information. For example, you can ask your cell phone to remind you to call someone back when you get to work, and your phone's location tracking will send you an alert the next time you arrive at your office.

Have Defined Goals

It's common to set broad goals like "Lose weight," "Spend more time with friends," or "Drink less." On the surface, these goals seem really beneficial. But it's hard to reach goals like these, in part because they're vague. How much weight should you lose? Does water weight count? What if you put on lean muscle weight? And when goals are so broad, there's no way to really measure progress. This can lead to a situation where you lose 15 pounds—a great accomplishment!—and then get discouraged because even though you're losing weight, you don't know if you're doing it quickly enough to be consistent with your goals.

In contrast, a defined goal has five specific criteria, summarized by the acronym SMART: Specific, Measurable, Attainable, Relevant, and Time-Limited. Having defined goals lets us know we're on track, and that's motivating.

When creating a defined goal, be as *specific* as possible: "Do homework" is vague, while "Write history paper" is more specific. **Measurable** means your goal has numbers in it—how much time you'll put into it, how often it will occur, etc. "Write" isn't measurable, but "Write for 90 minutes" or "Complete three pages" is. **Attainable** means it's only slightly more challenging than what you're currently doing. If you haven't studied in four months, it's unlikely you'll suddenly be able to breeze through your writing and research. While setting a goal like "Write paper in a single session" might lead to disappointment, something like "Write in 30-minute increments with 5-minute breaks" is more attainable. **Relevant** means that your goal matters to you, so think about why you're pursuing it. You've decided to focus on your history paper because doing well on this will bring up your grade for the semester, raising your GPA. And, finally, the goal needs to be **time-limited**, which means you'll set a deadline for yourself. "Write history paper" isn't time-limited, but "Complete three pages by Wednesday" is. All together, your SMART goal for writing the paper is "Write three pages of the history paper by Wednesday by working in 30-minute increments with 5-minute breaks so you can bring up your grade and raise your GPA."

Remind Yourself There Is No "Perfect Time"

In chapter 2, you learned that deluding yourself into thinking there will be a "perfect time" to get a task done contributes to procrastination. But in order to build the strong foundation you need to overcome procrastination, it's important to truly absorb this truth.

It's probably true that you're tired now, but will you actually be less tired tomorrow? And yeah, you don't feel like doing it right now, but will you suddenly be filled with motivation over the next few hours? Of course, you have better things to do—but don't you always? Maybe you don't have everything you need to complete the task, but can you get started with what you've got? And sure, you've got plenty of time to get it done, but would putting it off really help?

Waiting for some magical future moment when you suddenly have loads of time, energy, and motivation might leave you waiting forever. At the very least, it will keep you in the cycle of stressing yourself out to get things done at the last minute. So, go ahead and remind yourself there is no perfect time to do things you've been putting off.

Reframe the Rewards

When you approach a task you've been delaying, it starts to feel *especially* unpleasant. Getting the laundry folded doesn't feel like a big deal until it's been sitting in a pile on the couch for a week. But instead of focusing on how unpleasant it will feel to do the task, try to focus on how rewarding it will feel to get it done. *Doing* your taxes is awful, but having your taxes *done* feels awesome. This type of mindset shift is critical to overcoming procrastination.

Our brains naturally focus on the negative, the dangerous, and the unpleasant. This is a survival feature: It's safer to spend extra resources thinking about how you'll escape a burning building than it is to notice the pretty wall art while the fire alarm is blaring. But most of the time, we're not procrastinating on things related to survival. (In most cases, your brain won't even let you procrastinate on those things.) In these ordinary situations, it's okay to shift your focus from the escape route to the wall art, from how much work it will be to change your sheets to how amazing it will feel to slide into clean sheets. Be warned: Your brain is totally going to work against you and try to shift your focus back to the negative feelings when you try to do this. It takes extra (and repeated) effort to focus on the reward of pushing through those feelings, but the payoff is worth it.

Consider the Positives

You may sometimes procrastinate fun things—like calling friends or setting up happy hours—but most of the things we put off are unpleasant. When you're trying to complete a task that's objectively less fun than anything else you could be doing, you're going to need some good strategies for talking yourself through it. Make a list of the benefits of doing the task now. Yes, it's unpleasant/boring/tedious, but you probably also have some really good reasons to stop putting it off. Consider what those reasons are. How will it improve your situation, yourself, or your life to make progress on the goal? What kind of emotional rewards will you get for doing it? What opportunities might come your way if you move forward?

Don't just *think* through the positives—write them out. Our brains process information differently in writing, and writing takes more time than thinking, which gives our brains extra time to really consider and process an idea.

Seek Structure

One of the most important things you can do to start overcoming procrastination is set up a general schedule for your day—what time you get up, when you usually eat your meals, how you fit in work/school/studying, and what time you start winding down and going to sleep. Having a basic routine helps your brain predict when it will get fresh energy, which allows it to feel comfortable spending some fuel on motivating you. It also helps your brain predict when you'll need extra focus, so it can boost you with some bonus hormones and neurotransmitters when you need them. Having structure can be especially difficult when you have a variable schedule, but committing to getting up, going to bed, and eating meals at consistent times can make a monumental difference in your ability to get things done.

Many procrastinators really don't like structure or routine. In fact, some flat-out reject it. There are many reasons for that, but one is because it's unfamiliar and anything that's unfamiliar feels uncomfortable. Know that imposing some structure on your life will probably feel strange or uncomfortable at first. As with any other awkward situation, though, it will feel more comfortable as it becomes more familiar.

Make It as Easy as Possible

Your brain conserves energy as part of its strategy to keep you alive. Back in the days when food was scarce, humans had to be really cautious about expending energy because we never knew when we'd be able to replenish it. That's why your brain will encourage you to conserve energy whenever possible. The problem is that accomplishing goals, overcoming procrastination, and moving forward in your life is usually pretty difficult and energy-intensive, so your brain puts up a fight.

You can make this tendency work for you by making *not* procrastinating as easy as possible. Just as it's easier to choose celery sticks as a snack if you only have healthy food in your house, it's easier to choose to work when you don't have access to any procrastination temptations. Try to figure out what you use to procrastinate, and then see what you can do to eliminate those options. If you procrastinate by playing video games with your friends at night, tell them beforehand you've got a project to work on. If you procrastinate by watching TV with your partner, go to the library. Identify as many of the roadblocks to productivity as you can and make them difficult to access.

You know now that overcoming procrastination won't be easy or quick, but it's *definitely* possible and I'm here to help you with it. The next seven chapters are packed with evidence-based strategies you can use to address the root cause of your procrastination and start building better habits. Learning to be self-aware, defining your goals, and establishing structure will help you put these specific strategies into action. Remember, there will be setbacks along the way, so practice self-compassion as you encounter them and focus on the positives of taking action.

If you're anything like me (and everyone I know), your to-do list is essentially infinite, so it's important to figure out where to start. Let's dive into what the research says about the best way to prioritize your list.

CHAPTER FIVE

Prioritize

The first step in overcoming procrastination is deciding on a task to work on. This sounds simple but is surprisingly tricky. By definition, everything on your to-do list needs to get done, and there's actually a lot of brain processing involved in deciding what to prioritize. Our brains do some complex calculations to balance what objectively *needs* to get done with what we *want* to get done, as well as what we have the energy and resources to *actually* get done. What seems like a simple case of "first do this, then do that" is in reality pretty complicated at a neurological level. In this chapter, we'll talk about the basics of prioritizing effectively, and examine evidence-based strategies for putting your to-do list in order.

The Importance of Prioritizing

Prioritizing is the process of listing or rating goals, projects, or tasks in the order they need to be completed. In life, we're always prioritizing—we just don't always notice it. Choosing to hang out with your friends instead of going to your professor's office hours is prioritizing your social life over your education. For some people, this is pretty classic and obvious procrastination, stemming from failed prioritization. But for others, socializing is the right priority for them—maybe they've been neglecting their friendships, and making the choice to spend time with friends honors their goal to nurture those relationships. There's nothing inherently wrong with placing any one task in a higher priority than another. It all depends on what your personal goals are and what you believe you need to be working toward.

Effective Prioritizing

I haven't seen it, but your to-do list is definitely too long. Our brains can only handle a fairly small amount of information at a time, so you need to whittle your list down to something that's manageable for your brain. Ideally, you'll have one or two (*max* three) priorities per day. Anything more is overwhelming for you and your brain.

If you don't have an actual to-do list, start there. Keeping the list in your head ties up critical brain resources, so free up some RAM by writing things down. Our brains also process information differently in writing, so you can capitalize on that by actually writing out your list.

Right now, make a list of tasks, projects, deadlines, and appointments. Keep your list in a centralized location; try not to have 30 different lists all over the place. Add to this list any time something comes to mind. Now that you've got a list, use these evidence-based strategies for getting it in order.

The Eisenhower Matrix is a technique attributed to President Eisenhower and later popularized by Stephen R. Covey. This technique is supposedly based on a speech in which Eisenhower quoted a college president who said, "I have two kinds of problems, the urgent and the important. The urgent are not important, and the important are never urgent."

The goal is to separate urgency from importance. For each task on your list, decide whether it is urgent (requires immediate attention), important (connected to your values or your long-term goals), both, or neither.

	URGENT	NOT URGENT
IMPORTANT	Do Now	Schedule
NOT IMPORTANT	Delegate	Eliminate

Tasks that are both urgent and important come first. These include crises and problems needing immediate attention. Examples are work or school deadlines, health or weather emergencies, taxes, car trouble, or something affecting your income.

Tasks that are important but aren't urgent should be scheduled for later. Don't skip over the "schedule" part. These are things that will help you move toward your goals but don't necessarily have a deadline. Examples are learning new skills, starting a diet or exercise routine, improving your relationships, self-care, reading, budgeting, or taking a class.

The third priority level includes tasks that are urgent but aren't important to you. If possible, try to delegate these tasks; otherwise, make time for them after you prioritize the tasks above. Examples are extraneous meetings, most phone calls/emails/texts, and people who need favors. With respect to favors, usually they're urgent for the person needing the favor, but they're not necessarily important to you. Still, doing these things helps keep your relationships healthy, so it's valuable to make time for them if possible.

Finally, tasks that aren't urgent and don't help you progress toward your goals are the lowest priority and often can be eliminated. Examples include trying a new kickboxing class because your friend raved about it, even though you don't really care about kickboxing, or installing decorative lights in your backyard at your mother's suggestion, even though you don't mind the darkness. All your favorite time-wasters are also in this category: scrolling social media, watching YouTube videos, unnecessary shopping, watching TV. These sneaky "tasks" probably aren't actually on your to-do list (for good reason!). But when you tell yourself you'll call the pharmacy for your prescription refill right after you finish the next *Walking Dead* episode, Netflix has essentially joined your to-do list and is in this fourth category of tasks that can be eliminated.

ABC GROUPING

Another way of sorting your tasks is ABC grouping. The A group includes tasks that *must* get done. These are the highest-importance tasks that must be completed today or tomorrow. Work or school deadlines, bills, and chores could go in this group.

The B group includes tasks you *should* get done. These are less important or urgent than the A tasks, but still need to get done at some point. They also might be spread out a bit—they might be bigger projects that have some pieces that need to be completed relatively soon, while other pieces can be finished later. Things like routine medical checkups, meal prepping, family time, and creating a budget fit in this category.

The C group includes tasks that you *want* to get done, but aren't very important. This includes things like building your Pinterest dream home, putting together a photo album, planning your next vacation, or learning new recipes.

Once you group your tasks into A, B, and C groups, commit to doing all A tasks before you do any B tasks; then do all B tasks before you do any C tasks.

Urgency is a big part of how we decide what to prioritize. So, we need to know when things are "due" to assess how urgent they are. But many tasks have no deadline. There's no due date for mopping your kitchen floor, getting a Pap smear, or calling your grandma. Because of this, these tasks get pushed off in favor of your exam on Tuesday, the bill due tomorrow, and the video game sale that ends at midnight.

Combat this by setting deadlines for everything. Even if it's an arbitrary deadline, choose a date by which you'll complete each item on your list. If an item on your list has sub-parts, set deadlines for each of those smaller parts, too. Then, rank your list according to the deadlines. Maybe it's important to you to go back to school, but there's no real due date for completing your degree, so you keep putting it off. Prioritize by setting a date by which you want to gather information about how to re-enroll, and then set a date for registering for classes. When these dates are clearly established (and on your calendar!), they'll become more urgent and move up the priority list.

Sticking to self-imposed deadlines can be challenging because there aren't any external consequences to ignoring them. If you find yourself blowing off the deadlines you've set for yourself, try reminding yourself why that particular deadline matters. Instead of just writing "Research how to re-enroll" on your calendar for Saturday at 10 a.m., write "Research how to re-enroll at school—do it now so I won't miss spring enrollment again, so I can take a step to getting out of this terrible job, and so I can enjoy the pool this afternoon."

CUT ANYTHING THAT DOESN'T SUPPORT YOUR FUTURE GOALS

Unfortunately, we can't do everything we'd like to do, so we must choose where to direct our time and energy. Trim your list by eliminating tasks that don't directly support your goals.

The first step is getting clear on your goals. Goals related to school or work will probably come to you right away—maybe you want to finish your degree, get promoted, or develop certain skills to build your résumé. You also have goals in other areas of your life—they could be tied to philanthropy, politics/citizenship, spirituality, parenting, intimate relationships, family, friendships, health, personal growth, etc. Refer to chapter 4 (see page 45) for more details about how to define your goals.

Once you're certain about which goals you want to focus on, review your to-do list for items that aren't consistent with them. Then, consider eliminating those items. If you were planning on spending the weekend knitting your dog a sweater but don't have any goals related to knitting, sweaters, or your dog, then consider just buying the dog a sweater. You can get an awful lot done if you pare your activities down to those directly supporting what's important to you.

SORT BY ESTIMATED TIME TO COMPLETE

Once you've cut tasks that are unnecessary or don't support your goals, you can prioritize by sorting your list according to how long it takes to complete each item. In chapter 2, we talked about how we're really, really bad at estimating time. But we can't improve if we don't practice. Examine your list and guess how long each task will take. Then, prioritize based on how much time you have available. If you have 30 free minutes, you can prioritize tasks that can be completed in 30 minutes or less. If you have a block of a few hours, you can prioritize tasks requiring a larger chunk of time. Keep track of how long you're spending on each activity so you can improve your time-estimation skills. If you chronically underestimate how long activities take, remember to add a few minutes to your estimation until it becomes more accurate. If you chronically overestimate, remember that you can probably shave a few minutes off your estimation.

PRIORITIZE BY CONSEQUENCES

Another way to prioritize is by considering the consequences of completing or delaying the task. Tasks with the highest priority should be those that come with serious consequences if they're delayed—getting reprimanded at work, getting in a fight with your spouse, becoming ill, losing a significant amount of money, etc. Next should be tasks with milder consequences—if you delay them, people might become frustrated with you or inconvenienced, there might be a small fine, something might become slightly damaged, etc. The next group includes tasks that would be nice to complete but have few consequences if you don't. This would cover things like organizing your closets, repainting your bedroom, or visiting with your neighbors. The last group includes tasks that can be eliminated without any consequences, like taking up a new hobby you're indifferent to or starting a new television show just because your friends are watching. This group also includes all the time-wasters we do even though they aren't actually on the official to-do list, like playing video games too much, primping in the mirror, spending too much time reading the news, and snacking (snacking monopolizes a surprising amount of time and productivity, by the way).

PRIORITIZE BY ESTIMATED EFFORT

You can also prioritize your tasks by how much effort you think the tasks will take. Be careful here! We're prone to procrastinate (i.e., de-prioritize) the tasks requiring the most effort. We tell ourselves we don't have enough energy, time, or resources to engage and procrastinate instead. The strategy here isn't simply to do the tasks requiring the least effort first and then save the higher-effort tasks for later. It's also not to do all the high-effort tasks first and the low-effort ones last.

Instead, this approach is about balancing the high- and low-energy tasks. Each day, choose one high-effort task and then spend the rest of your time working on tasks requiring less effort. This approach ensures the high-effort tasks won't get pushed aside. It also helps you make sure you're balancing your energy output—neither depleting yourself by completing a bunch of high-effort tasks at the last minute, nor indulging yourself by just doing a bunch of easier things. It's about spreading out your energy as much as spreading out the workload.

PRIORITIZE BY IMPACT ON YOUR QUALITY OF LIFE

Quality of life is your overall state of well-being; it's how healthy, comfortable, and satisfied you are. Prioritize your to-do list by analyzing how each task will impact your quality of life.

The question to ask yourself is, "Will this task make my life easier?" Will spending an hour reading Reddit threads make your life easier? Probably not. Would spending that same hour getting your oil changed make your life easier? Absolutely. Will spending a half hour picking out new holiday decorations make your life easier? Maybe cuter, but not easier. Would spending that half hour teaching your dog to come when she's called make your life easier? Guaranteed.

Warning! In chapter 2, you learned that procrastinators prioritize how they feel *right now*, with less focus on how they'll feel or what they'll need in the future. Practice focusing on your *long-term* quality of life, rather than your happiness and satisfaction in the moment.

Priorities are very personal. There's no "right" or "wrong" way to set your priorities, as long as they reflect your personal values and goals. But once you've created your to-do list and prioritized it, you're not finished yet. Your next step is to motivate yourself to work on the list. So let's start working on how to build motivation.

CHAPTER SIX

Find Motivation

One of the biggest concerns I hear from my clients is, "I just can't find the motivation to [insert task they've previously said they want to do]." We spend much of our lives trying to motivate ourselves to do unpleasant but important tasks, but that doesn't mean it's an easy thing to do. And if you're trying to overcome procrastination, motivating yourself to get started and to choose a harder or more tedious task over an easier or more pleasant one will be one of your greatest challenges. But that doesn't mean it's impossible. Let's start by figuring out what motivation is and where it comes from; then we'll take a look at evidence-based strategies for getting motivated.

What Is Motivation and Where Does It Come From?

Motivation is what helps us change ourselves, our situation, or our environment. All animals have motivation; it's what stimulates them to find food, a safe place to sleep, and a mate.

Contrary to popular belief, motivation isn't a static thing that you either do or don't have. It comes and goes. All animals appear to be motivated to secure food, safety, and sex, but basically no one wants these things all the time. As humans, we're motivated by far more than basic survival needs, but even still, we don't pursue social acceptance, fast cars, or fancy jewelry all the time. Motivation is in part a specific drive to do a specific action at a specific time, and it's highly influenced by what's going on *right now*. For example, people love eating, but when we've just loaded up at the buffet, we're less motivated to seek out food than if we haven't eaten in a while.

As with procrastination, motivation interacts with our emotions. For example, we're motivated to avoid pain. When we feel pain, we're motivated to stop what we're doing to end the pain. We're also motivated to increase comfort and happiness, which influences us to choose simple, immediate pleasures instead of making rational calculations that will help us pursue long-term goals. So, you might experience motivation in situations that feel good or have the potential to feel good but not in situations that don't feel so good in the moment.

The Importance of Motivation

Motivation is critically important for animal survival, so it's hardwired into our brains. Everyone's got motivation, but we might not necessarily channel it in the right direction. For example, we may feel motivated to learn the latest dance craze but not how to hem a pair of pants.

This occurs because we experience multiple conflicting motivations at once. We might be motivated to cook a healthy meal at the same time we're motivated to walk the dog, and our brains must choose between these competing tasks because we can only do one thing at any given time. Motivation is what helps us choose among all the things we *could* be doing in any given moment.

Another reason we find ourselves lacking motivation is because it follows what we want. We tell ourselves we want to eat healthy; but when we're honest with ourselves, we want *to want* to eat healthy. Big difference. Our motivation follows what we actually want, not what we wish we wanted. This combination of having to choose between multiple competing desires and being motivated by what we *actually* want can make it really difficult for us to do necessary but unpleasant tasks.

Find Your Motivation

To tackle your procrastination, you must solve this motivational problem. Psychologically, your motivation will direct you toward simple things that feel good now and away from complicated things that feel cumbersome. In other words, it will encourage you to procrastinate. Look back at your goals (chapter 4, see page 54) and your values to remind yourself of where you're headed. The key to motivation is to commit to those goals 100 percent. You'll know you're 100-percent committed when you're willing to feel uncomfortable in order to keep working on the goal or when you keep working toward it even on the days when you don't feel like it. Even a tiny reduction in your commitment (say, down to 99 percent) means every time you think about working toward your goals, you must ask yourself whether today is one of the times you'll move forward or one of the times you'll procrastinate. Making this decision every single time drains the brain resources you need to get tasks started. That sets you up for failure, which decreases your confidence that you can follow through with your goals, which decreases your motivation. The solution: Commit 100 percent, watch yourself follow through, build your confidence along the way, and build your motivation to continue.

Once you've committed, use the evidence-based strategies in this chapter to redirect your efforts in a valued direction. At first, you may not be especially motivated to go to the gym, eat celery, or write a weekly budget. But once you've committed 100 percent and established new habits, your motivation will follow. For example, once people stop smoking, their cravings for cigarettes diminish substantially and they feel more motivated to keep not smoking. Making choices that are more consistent with your long-term goals will be difficult at first, but it will become easier once you gain momentum. Once you've committed to a goal, focus more on the momentum of your actions than your motivation, then use these strategies to help keep your momentum alive.

WHAT FUTURE WOULD YOU WANT?

Find motivation by deliberately asking yourself what Future You would want (Hershfield, 2011). This question seems like it'd be unnecessary, but as we discussed in chapter 2, our brains are predisposed to think about the present moment, with substantially less concern about the future. I mean, it makes sense: If I don't survive this moment, I don't need to be concerned with any future moments. But when we're fortunate enough to not really have our survival threatened on a regular basis, it behooves us to refocus a smidge more on the future.

When you're considering how you should spend your time, ask yourself, "What would Future Me want?" Would Future You want you to spend another half hour watching unboxing videos on YouTube, or would Future You prefer that you spent that half hour reading a book to your kid? You will most likely have a very clear idea of what Future You would want, but it's important to deliberately ask yourself, because your brain definitely won't ask this question by itself. Use the answer to take action.

REVIEW YOUR SOCIAL CALENDAR

Many people convince themselves to procrastinate by thinking that if they take care of the task now, they'll miss out on fun. For example, "If I do the laundry, I'll miss out on this cool video game my friends are all playing online right now."

Build motivation by using that thought process to your advantage—flip it upside down and remind yourself what you'll miss out on if you delay. Get out your social calendar and see what's scheduled: You've got a happy hour, a book club meeting, a date night, and a concert coming up this week. If you don't complete that work project today, you'll need to skip one of those events in order to finish the project by Friday. Use that information to push yourself to get the task done now.

If social events aren't especially motivating to you, review your schedule of other pleasurable events. You've got antiquing on Saturday morning, a hike on Sunday, and *The Bachelor* on Monday; if you postpone cleaning the house now, you might miss one of those events. In other words, rather than using fun as an excuse *to* procrastinate, you can use fun as a reason to *not* procrastinate.

REMEMBER, THEN DO

"Remember, then do" means as soon as you remember something you've been meaning to do, do it right away. And I mean *right away*. Within just a few seconds, your brain will start talking you out of doing it, so capitalize on that brief moment before your brain starts to override your decision. If you walk by the kitchen and see a plate that needs to go in the dishwasher, don't add it to your to-do list; just do this quick task immediately.

This strategy prevents tiny tasks from accumulating on your to-do list. You won't waste any brainpower trying to remember to do them later. Plus, if you postpone until later, you'll need to muster motivation, which is really difficult to apply to tedious or unenjoyable tasks. Doing it immediately circumvents the need for motivation.

VISUALIZE YOURSELF COMPLETING THE TASK

Visualization is an extremely powerful feature of human brains. Athletes use visualization to run a play before they hit the field, painters use it to plan a piece before paint hits the canvas, and chess players use it to predict their opponents' moves. It's basically a practice run for your brain, and, as with anything, practicing makes us more successful. While your brain is processing this practice run, it's creating intention and motivation to help you follow through with the real deal.

Here's how it works: Say you want to go to the gym on your way home from work today, but history tells you that you're more likely to swing through the drive-thru on your way home to the recliner. Using visualization means you picture yourself doing the task, step by step, in your mind's eye. You start with the very first step, in this case getting in your car after work. You then envision yourself driving to the gym, parking, checking in, changing your clothes, working out, getting back in your car, and pulling into your driveway. Take your time with the visualization—the more realistic it is, the more effective it is. By giving your brain a trial run, you're almost tricking it into thinking this is already something you do routinely, making it easier.

USE TEMPTATION BUNDLING

Another way to build motivation is to pair something you don't want to do (i.e., something you'd rather procrastinate) with something you *like* doing. By bundling an unpleasant task with something more tempting, we can capitalize on our motivation for the more tempting task and use that to complete the less tempting task. This is called temptation bundling or impulse pairing.

Maybe you're a habitual procrastinator when it comes to studying for exams, but you really love talking to people. Setting up a study group pairs something you like (socializing) with something you'd ordinarily procrastinate (studying). It's a bit more motivating to engage with the material in a study group than it would be if you were sitting in the library by yourself. This is all about playing with the emotional component. The challenge is to find something that feels good *now* and pair it with something that doesn't feel so good but is important. Socializing feels good now; studying doesn't, but it's important. Bundling those two things together can help you apply your motivation for socializing to complete a different task.

EXAMINE THE ADVANTAGES AND DISADVANTAGES

Much of the human brain's motivational process happens unconsciously. We assess our goals and feelings and then decide on actions in a split second. Slowing this process down can help us make decisions more aligned with our long-term goals. Do this by taking a few minutes to write down (on paper, not in your head) the advantages and disadvantages of doing a task now versus putting it off.

Sometimes, delaying a task has legitimate advantages—maybe you'll get more information about a school assignment, someone will be available to help you later, or the weather will be more conducive to getting the yard work done. Examining all four quadrants gives your brain ample time and opportunity to consider your short-term needs *and* your long-term goals and make a full rational consideration instead of jumping to what's easiest. This will build motivation for the harder, more important tasks.

	ADVANTAGES	DISADVANTAGES
DO IT NOW		
POSTPONE		

KEEP A "DONE" LIST

The problem with to-do lists is that they never end. Seriously—on my death bed, I will still have a list of things I need to get done. Focusing on how much there still is to do can be discouraging and demotivating, but focusing on what has already been done can be encouraging and motivating. Check or cross items off your to-do list—it's psychologically satisfying. And keep a list of what you've already accomplished. It's a way of taking a moment to give yourself credit for work you've done, which will motivate you as you move on to new tasks.

Motivation is directly connected to what we want. But sometimes, we forget what we *really* want, because we also want something else. Maybe you want to pay off some debt, but you also want new patio furniture. It's important to take some time to remind yourself of what your goals really are and what you really want for yourself.

The key is to connect tasks to your life goals. Maybe the task is reading this book; that can be connected to your broader goal of learning how to overcome procrastination, which will take you toward your life goal of completing your degree and earning a better living to support your family. Or maybe the task is mopping the floor; that can be connected to your broader goal of demonstrating life skills to your children, which will take you toward your life goal of raising responsible humans.

Any task important enough to be on your to-do list should be connected in some way to your personal goals. Our brains don't automatically connect those dots, so taking a few moments to figure out how they relate can really make a difference for building motivation to do otherwise mundane tasks.

So, now that you know how to prioritize your list and how to get motivated to accomplish what's on it, it's time to actually get started on those tasks. Prepare yourself: This is the hardest part. But even though it is hard, it is absolutely doable. Let's talk about how you'll get started.

CHAPTER SEVEN

Get Started

It's surprisingly difficult to get started. It seems like once we decide what we want to do, we should just be able to do it. But as you've discovered, it's not that simple. Fortunately, psychologists have discovered a lot about why getting started can be such a struggle. Knowing what the psychological barriers are gives us some hints about strategies we can use to overcome them. In this chapter, we'll look at those evidence-based strategies.

Sometimes It's Hard to Get Started

We all have trouble getting new things started. But the brain processes involved in initiating tasks are often not as well-developed in procrastinators, so they're at a clear disadvantage when they try to begin a new project. Take Nathaniel as an example. Nathaniel's family outgrew their home once their second child was born. Building an extra bedroom was clearly important to him: He valued ensuring his children grew up with more privileges than he'd had. But he just couldn't get started on the project. His original goal was to complete the bedroom before the baby was born, but before he knew it, the baby was walking and he still hadn't started.

When Nathaniel tried to get started on the bedroom, he felt disorganized with the process, intimidated by the magnitude of the project, and resentful that building the room was his responsibility. To find relief from these feelings, he delayed the project and buried himself in his phone, an activity that made him feel confident and self-assured. Approaching any new task, even if it's one you feel relatively confident about, will generate feelings: You might feel unsure, impatient, intimidated, drained, directionless, or uncomfortable. It will also generate doubts about whether you'll make mistakes, whether you'll still have time for fun and relaxation, and whether expectations will increase if you do the task well. Getting started requires that you have a plan for managing those feelings and thoughts.

The Key to Getting Started

The key to getting started is recognizing that it won't be easy. Waiting for a moment when all the stars align and suddenly there's nothing in the world you'd rather do than build a bedroom is fruitless. We must be honest with ourselves about that and develop a strategy for managing the thoughts and feelings that arise when we do difficult things.

We struggle to get started because, rather than working on our coping strategies, we ignore those difficult feelings and thoughts and pretend they're not there. Ignoring feelings is about as effective as ignoring the mosquito flying around your living room—it's still there, and it still might bite you. If you don't acknowledge and deal with your feelings, they'll continue to disrupt your process and motivate you to procrastinate. But once you appreciate that managing your feelings is part of overcoming procrastination, you can use the following evidence-based strategies to get your tasks started.

This strategy is a cornerstone of cognitive behavioral therapy (CBT), one of the most widely researched and evidence-based psychological interventions for just about every mental health condition, from depression to anxiety to ADHD. It's all about catching the unhelpful thoughts diverting you from getting started on tasks. This is one of my absolute favorite strategies, because the evidence base for it is so strong. You should highlight this one, put some stars next to it, and practice it a hundred times.

When you try to start a task, you'll have unhelpful thoughts that interfere with actually getting it started. Here are some examples:

I'm too tired/anxious/sad/stressed/etc. to work on this.

I can do it tomorrow.

I can't finish on time anyway, so what's the point? It's not that important, so it can wait.

I don't have enough time to do it.

Once I finish this, I'll work on that.

I don't feel like working on it right now.

Catch those thoughts and investigate them. Pretend you're a scientist and treat the thoughts as hypotheses. Then, run an experiment to see if the hypotheses are true.

Hypothesis: I'm too tired to fill out this job application tonight.

Evidence Supporting Hypothesis: I got up early today. I had a lot of meetings today. My kids are extra wild today.

Evidence Contradicting Hypothesis: Most of the application is mindless demographic information. I'll be awake for a few more hours anyway. I've succeeded at many things in my life despite being tired.

Finally, summarize what you learned into a response to the original hypothesis.

Rational Response: It's true I'm tired, but that doesn't mean I can't get started with the application. Plus, I've done many things in my life well despite being tired.

Ordinarily, you hear yourself say, "I'm too tired," accept that as fact, and then procrastinate. The important part here is to catch the unhelpful thoughts rather than ignoring them, and then challenge them to see if they're true. Often, you'll find serious inaccuracies in the excuses you're making to procrastinate.

USE A SCHEDULE OR AN UNSCHEDULE

You know what a schedule is—it's a list of events or activities that you plan to do at a certain time. Research consistently shows that scheduled activities are more likely to happen than activities that aren't scheduled. So, being too flexible and winging it with your tasks or goals can contribute to procrastination. Deciding on a time to pay your bills, open your mail, make a medical appointment, or arrange a social event makes it significantly more likely that you will actually start those tasks. Use a planner or a calendar app to schedule activities, and set an alarm or reminder to cue yourself to stick to the schedule. Even if it's an activity that doesn't need to occur at a specific time, like grocery shopping, try assigning a time for yourself anyway (like 11 a.m. on Saturday) to help yourself get started on tasks.

Procrastinators are almost always allergic to schedules, so let me introduce you to an alternative: the unschedule. An unschedule starts with all the scheduled tasks in your life—your work schedule, your class schedule, your regular appointments, your sleep schedule, your meal schedule, your Thursday night bar trivia, anything you do on a regular basis. Between those events are blank spaces. That's where the unschedule lives. These blank spaces are your opportunities for all the things you've been procrastinating. Ordinarily, that blank space just disappears—we watch TV, play on our phones, chat with our coworkers, and snooze with it. But you can use that blank space to get started on tasks. Pair the blank space in your unschedule with your to-do list (chapter 5, page 59) and loosely schedule appointments with yourself to get tasks done during those spaces.

CHUNK YOUR TASKS

It is especially hard to get started on big or overwhelming tasks. Tasks like "Study for history exam," "Pack up the house to move," or "Lose 25 pounds" are so monumental that they inevitably trigger some majorly distressing emotions, which are then followed by procrastination. "Chunking" your tasks involves breaking the tasks into components and doing one "chunk" or section at a time. For example, say your task is to pack the house so you can move. You can chunk this into rooms and then take each room in chunks: Start with the bedroom closet, then move to the junk hidden under the bed, then pack up the night stands, then throw the stuff from the dresser into a box. Once you throw the wall decorations in a bag, your bedroom chunk is complete and it's time to move on to the bathroom chunk. Each room and each area of a room can be a single chunk.

USE MOMENTUM

Momentum is a powerful resource in getting started. It's often hard to get the ball rolling, but once it's rolling, it's easier to keep it going. Start with an energizing task and then quickly switch to another task you've been putting off. Ideally, the two tasks should be somewhat related. For example, maybe you're procrastinating on getting to the gym. Start by stretching or walking your dog, and then use the momentum from that physical activity to launch yourself into the more daunting task.

The key to this technique is to be able to distinguish between draining and energizing activities. If you're not sure what energizes you, collect some data for yourself by watching your energy level before and after common activities in your life. You might be surprised because many things we do to "relax"—like watching TV and scrolling social media—actually don't restore our energy at all. Energizing activities include things like going for a walk, playing with your kids or pets, exercising, and volunteering. Use the momentum from those energizing tasks to transition yourself into the more draining tasks you procrastinate.

DO THE EASIEST OR HARDEST FIRST

Get started on tasks by targeting the easiest part or task first. Once you've conquered a minimal amount of discomfort by doing a relatively easy task, you show yourself that you're ready to conquer a tiny bit more discomfort with a harder task. This works especially well with quick, easy items on your to-do list: loading the dishwasher, checking the mail, or getting out a fresh toothbrush. Once you've accomplished those tasks, you can use that momentum to tackle harder items.

An alternative is to do the opposite: Target the hardest part or task first. If you've been dreading something, getting that major discomfort out of the way helps all the other tasks on the list seem much more manageable. This works especially well for quick but really unpleasant items on your to-do list: cleaning the toilet, making a tough phone call, or handing in your letter of resignation. Once you've accomplished these tasks, you'll have the confidence to tackle the easier items.

SET A TIME LIMIT

One of the excuses we use to avoid getting started on tasks is that we'll miss out on other, more enjoyable things if we do them. You can overcome that thought process by setting a time limit for engaging with a task. The length of time is arbitrary, but the commitment to a *specific* number of minutes is crucial. If you commit to doing something for a specific length of time, it's imperative that you do it for the whole time, no more and no less. You need to be able to trust yourself that if you say you're only going to do something for 15 minutes, you'll keep your word. If there's even a *hint* of expectation in the back of your mind that you might keep going after the time limit is up, it'll be hard to get started—you're too smart to trick yourself into this!

Commit to engaging with the task for a certain time limit, and then return to whatever it is you would have otherwise procrastinated with. Even if 15 minutes of work seems too small to make a difference, it's still 15 more minutes than you had been doing before. And it's actually amazing what you can accomplish with 15 minutes of dedicated time (walk a mile, read nine pages, wash the dishes, etc.).

A related time-keeping approach is to do a task for just five minutes. Again, the number of minutes is arbitrary, but choose a manageable and tolerable amount of time. Unlike the "set a time limit" approach, this approach allows you to renew your time. So, you'll commit to working on a task for just five minutes. At the end of that time, decide whether you'd like to commit to another five minutes or move on to another activity. Continue until you decide you would prefer to move on. Initially, five minutes may be all you can tolerate. But as you practice this strategy, you'll likely be able to extend the time you engage with difficult, tedious, or unpleasant tasks. And once you've got the ball rolling for five minutes, you'll amaze yourself at how much easier it gets to keep going.

Just like with the "set a time limit" approach, this isn't about tricking yourself into spending time on a task. This is about honestly making a decision to tackle a task in small five-minute chunks of time and giving yourself an honest option to discontinue the task at five-minute intervals.

REVIEW YOUR REGRETS

We've all got a long list of regrets—drunk texting an ex, lower back tattoos, bangs. But some things in life are almost impossible to regret. Things like going for a walk, spending extra time with people you love, eating a healthy meal, thanking someone, recycling, drinking water, exercising . . . the list is endless, really. You know what's also impossible to regret? Getting started on something you've been putting off. Think about it: How many times have you regretted finishing something early, being extra-prepared for a test, or having a head start on a project? Now consider the opposite: How many times have you regretted your decision to procrastinate? My guess is that you've regretted it often, and that's why you started reading this book to begin with. Taking this mindset and remembering that it's nearly impossible to regret getting started (but very easy to regret starting late) can help you get over the hump of starting something new.

Once you've started a task, it's easy to get distracted. That's why your next challenge is staying focused on what you're doing. Let's figure out some methods for making sure you follow through.

CHAPTER EIGHT

Focus

By this point, you've learned how to prioritize, you've dedicated yourself to your goals as a way of motivating action, and you've gotten started on the tasks you want to complete. Now, it's time to tackle the next hurdle: staying focused. This can be a surprisingly difficult part of the journey. Even after you put all that effort into feeling motivated and getting started, it's still easy to get distracted from your target. Certain people are more prone to distractibility than others, so let's start with a review of what makes focus an issue for certain people, and then launch into evidence-based strategies for improving focus.

Getting and Staying Focused

Like many jobs, Grace's job involved a lot of boring, tedious documentation. And it was incredibly difficult for her to stay focused. At any given moment, she'd have 18 tabs open on her web browser, all representing single moments of curiosity that accumulated into hours of lost productivity. The documentation that should have taken her about an hour of dedicated focus per day ended up taking over much of her life. And the more time she spent trying to complete her paperwork, the more fatigued she became and the harder it was to focus. It was a vicious cycle.

To simplify a very complex issue, attention is your ability to concentrate on one thing (a thought, a task, a sensation, etc.) while you ignore everything else you could be concentrating on at the same time.

Difficulty concentrating is a symptom of nearly all mental health conditions. The brain changes that occur when people are depressed or anxious, for example, interfere with their ability to focus their attention, making things like reading a book, having a conversation with a friend, or even watching a television show much more difficult. But problems with attention and focus are *especially* problematic for people who have ADHD. ADHD can cause people to be forgetful, lose things, and get distracted or sidetracked easily—all of which make sustaining focus very difficult.

Sustained Focus

Though problems with attention, concentration, and focus are brain-based, that doesn't mean they're permanent or that they can only be changed with medication. Just as biceps curls can strengthen your arm muscles, stimulating the part of your brain involved in focus helps strengthen that area. Even for people with mental health conditions, including ADHD, focus can be practiced and improved. But, of course, you can't do just one biceps curl every now and then and expect to get stronger—repetition and progressively increasing the challenge are important components of building strength. The same is true for building focus. It's important to challenge yourself to focus, do it repeatedly, and push yourself over time to increase the duration and intensity.

In that spirit, this chapter introduces strategies to get and stay focused. These techniques are designed to help you find when you're best able to focus, learn how to stay engaged with a task longer so you have the opportunity to exercise your brain, and build your ability to increase your focus over time. Before we begin, though, the most important component of focus is a solid foundation of physical health. Fatigue, hunger, and malnutrition all interfere with your ability to focus, so be sure to get enough sleep, exercise, and healthy food to set your brain up for success. Then, try these interventions to build your focus.

KNOW YOUR PRIME TIME TO FOCUS

Your ability to focus varies on a 24-hour cycle called your circadian rhythm. Your circadian rhythm affects a huge number of biological processes, including sleep, appetite, and body temperature. Your attention is also on that list. For most people, attention is poorest in the middle of the night and in the early morning hours, better around noon, and best in the afternoon and evening.

But individual differences exist in our circadian rhythms, so it's important to determine when your own attention is strongest. Even if you don't think you're a morning person, try to see how your focus is in the morning. This can change with age, so the fact that you couldn't concentrate well in the morning when you were in college doesn't necessarily mean that's still true today.

Once you know when your attention is strongest, plan to do the tasks requiring the most focus during that time frame. Things like reading, paying bills, or learning a new hobby should be in that category. Tasks like folding laundry, running errands, and spending time with others require less attention, so save them for the time of day when it's harder for you to focus.

ADJUST YOUR ENVIRONMENT

In addition to establishing your prime time for concentrating, it's also important to determine your prime space. Our brains are very sensitive to our environments. That's why you get sleepy when you slide into bed, why you feel excited at an amusement park, and why you crave funnel cakes at the state fair. When your brain is in a physical space it associates with relaxation or fun, it will be more prone to distraction and resistant to focused attention. Likewise, when your brain is in a physical space it associates with hard, concentrated work, it will be more prone to help you stay focused.

Use this to your advantage by creating a dedicated space for focused work. If you work well from home, create a home office or an area reserved for concentrating. If you don't work well from home, experiment with other spaces—libraries, coffee shops, your workplace, bookstores, and parks can all be good spaces to concentrate. As you're choosing a space, consider your proximity to temptation. The library might not be the best choice if you're susceptible to getting distracted by books, and you might want to avoid the coffee shop if you find yourself getting involved in every conversation you overhear. If you work in a bustling office, adjust your environment to be more focus-friendly by requesting a desk near a wall rather than in the middle of the room, using the tallest partitions you're permitted around your desk, and minimizing decorations and clutter in your workspace.

At your workspace, surround yourself with cues that confirm your goals. Make a vision board, post a sticky note, or tape a picture to your desk reminding you why studying for this one exam is so important. It could be that it's helping you complete your degree so you can live independently, get a great job, or provide for your family. The specific reason doesn't matter; all that matters is that it's important to you.

REMOVE DISTRACTIONS

An incredibly important part of getting and staying focused is managing the things that could compromise that focus. You likely already know that you should eliminate the obvious distractions, like people, television, and games—of course it's harder to focus on your physics homework if your roommates are playing loud video games right next to you. But it's also important to remove (or remove yourself from) less obvious distractions, like your cat, your phone, email, or snacks. Removing distractions begins with keeping track of what's really distracting you (remember when we talked about self-awareness in chapter 4?) and then getting creative about how to distance yourself from those temptations. Here are a few ideas to start with.

Turn off all the extra screens (phone, TV, computer) around you, as your brain is attracted to their light and will get distracted. Put your phone in airplane mode so you can't be distracted by phone calls, texts, and notifications. If you're worried about missing an emergency call, use the "do not disturb" mode and set exceptions only for your closest family members and loved ones. Tell them you're working on something important, and ask them to please only contact you in an emergency.

Email is one of the sneakiest distractions around, so mute your Gmail with Inbox Pause or use a similar app to silence email notifications while you're working. If you're working on a computer, use an app or extension to block distracting websites. If you don't need the internet for your task but find yourself getting distracted by websites, unplug your router or temporarily disable your Wi-Fi connection.

WRITE DISTRACTIONS DOWN FOR LATER

No matter how effectively you remove distractions from your environment, there's still the possibility of becoming distracted by your own mind. If you find your thoughts pulling your focus, try a "distractibility delay," a technique for training your brain to focus for increasingly longer periods of time.

Determine an amount of time you want to work on a task before you take a break—say, 15 minutes. During those 15 minutes, make a note of any distractions that come up. These could be thoughts or ideas you have or other things you need to do. For example, while you're studying for a history exam, you have the thought that you'd rather be starving on a deserted island than studying. You then find yourself wondering whether old episodes of *Survivor* are online and get sucked into a YouTube vortex of the best *Survivor* moments. Rather than following up on these distractions in the moment, write down the questions, ideas, to-do list items, or other distractions that come up while you're working, and re-examine them when you're no longer in the middle of a task. Delaying your distractibility will help you stay focused on what you're doing and train your brain to stay focused for longer periods of time.

Limit extraneous noise, like the TV, to enhance your focus. For sounds you can't eliminate (like your roommate talking in the next room or the dog barking next door), try noise-cancelling headphones.

Once you've tried eliminating sounds, experiment with adding other sounds in. While unpredictable noise can be distracting, certain sounds, like white noise and pink noise, have been repeatedly shown to enhance attention (Helps, Bamford, Sonuga-Barke, and Söderlund, 2014). Our brains process music differently than other sounds, so you can listen to your favorite songs while you work, using the tempo and energy of the music to enhance your focus. It may be helpful to play calming instrumental music (e.g., elevator music, classical music) to reduce anxiety and maintain focus during some tasks. For other tasks, high-energy music (e.g., techno or other types of electronic dance music) could be helpful. Experiment to see what works best for you.

Binaural beats may also enhance attention. Binaural beats are a specific type of music where the listener hears two different sounds simultaneously, one in each ear. One sound is slightly higher in pitch than the other, which creates the illusion of hearing three sounds. This sounds gimmicky, but there's actually scientific evidence that binaural beats make your brain process information differently, which enhances attention and concentration in some people. Scientists are still trying to understand exactly how, why, for whom, and in what circumstances binaural beats are effective, but at the very least there's evidence they are calming, and having a calmer brain increases the ability to focus. Remember to use headphones if you use this strategy to make sure the separate sounds are being played to each ear.

TAKE BREAKS

You have a finite amount of attentional resources. Attention starts to wane within the first few minutes of starting a task. Once you start drifting off, you can sometimes get yourself refocused, but the period of time you can refocus for gets shorter and shorter as you go on. Taking breaks allows your brain time to catch up and replenish the energy it spent trying to help you focus. Giving your brain a few minutes to refuel can help you get refocused and stay focused longer. Every 15 minutes, take a three-minute break. After you've had three three-minute breaks, take a 15-minute break. Continue alternating three

three-minute breaks and one 15-minute break for every 15 minutes you work. While you're on your break, do something to bring more oxygen to your brain: breathing exercises, jumping jacks, or a quick meditation work well to replenish focus.

If you can't focus for 15 minutes at first, break the task down. Maybe you can only focus for 10 minutes, or five, or one. Start there, take a short break (aim for about 20 percent of the amount of time you focused), and then start again.

One challenge with taking breaks is getting yourself back on task when the break is done. Try setting a timer for each break so you'll be reminded to get back to work.

USE TIMERS

Timers can be a great resource for staying focused. As I just mentioned, you can use them to measure your breaks, but you can also use them to build self-awareness regarding whether you're on task. At regular intervals, your timer will beep, allowing you to examine where you are with your work. Maybe you started working on a job application, but a few minutes later, you're on a totally unrelated internet forum. When your timer goes off, you'll realize it's time to get back on task. Having the timer go off regularly will help keep those distractions from taking over your entire day, which means you'll spend more time focused on your goal and make more progress.

In deciding how often the timer should go off, consider how often you get distracted. Start by making an educated guess about how long you can stay focused (say, 15 minutes). Then, if the alarm goes off and you realize you've been off task for several minutes, you can shorten the duration for the next cycle. Or, if you're still on task and going strong, you could try lengthening the duration. Try using an old-fashioned kitchen timer for this, as they're easy to reset and don't present the same temptation for distraction that your phone does.

Before you even try to get focused on a task, it's important to set yourself up for success. Set aside 5 to 10 minutes before you start working to set up your space and organize your time. Adjust your environment, remove external distractions, get some paper to write down your internal distractions for later, set up your white noise, music, or binaural beats, and get out your kitchen timer.

Then, make a plan for how you'll tackle the task. What's your specific goal to accomplish, and how will you accomplish it? If you're sitting down to study, decide what classes you'll study for, what materials you'll need, and what you'll read or review. If you're paying bills, make a list of which bills you need to pay. If you're fixing something around the house, make a plan for exactly how you'll fix it and try to think of everything you'll need.

Spending just a few minutes getting your time and your space organized will allow you to stay focused on the actual task itself once you start working.

Now you know some proven techniques to help you get focused and stay focused on your goals, which is a huge part of overcoming procrastination. But an equally important part is managing the emotions that come up when you try to approach a task that's boring, unpleasant, tedious, difficult, or intimidating. Those feelings make us want to avoid tasks that are otherwise important, making us feel even worse in the end. Let's get to work on some strategies for overcoming avoidance.

CHAPTER NINE

Overcome Avoidance

Though we've already discussed techniques for motivating yourself and focusing, you actually need two sets of skills to get started on a task: behavioral skills (like those from chapter 7) that help you take actions and emotional skills that help you manage the feelings that come up when you start something new. These emotional skills help you overcome avoidance, which is one of the biggest issues in procrastination. Sometimes avoidance is about avoiding tasks, sometimes it's about avoiding decisions, but mostly, it's about avoiding feelings. No matter what form avoidance takes in your life, the techniques in this chapter are designed to help you overcome it and move forward with your goals.

What Is Avoidance?

At its root, procrastination is about avoiding tasks or decisions because they feel uncomfortable in some way—because they're monotonous, challenging, disorganized, gross, intimidating, confusing, or lonely. In fact, procrastination is more about avoiding those feelings than it is about avoiding the task itself.

These feelings come in at two different points in time: when we're actually *doing* the task and when we *think about* doing the task. Because we're motivated to minimize feelings of discomfort, we will sometimes choose to avoid as a way of managing those feelings. For example, if I decide not to give the dog a bath tonight, I feel relieved right now (I don't have to dread giving the dog a bath later) and I know I'll feel relieved tonight, too (because I won't have to do the unpleasant task).

Avoidance is extremely common among people with anxiety. Your brain is wired to make you avoid what scares you because it assumes whatever you fear is legitimately life-threatening. Staying away means you're staying alive. But the biggest thing people with anxiety avoid is uncertainty. By taking no action and making no change, they eliminate uncertainty, which relieves anxiety. Avoidance is also common in depression, where maintaining the status quo conserves energy and avoiding decisions reduces the likelihood of regret.

Mia had frequent panic attacks and was terrified of triggering future ones. Seeking an easy way to manage her panic disorder, she avoided all sorts of things she believed might set off a panic attack: exercising, attending client meetings, driving on the freeway. She became physically unhealthy, missed opportunities to grow her business, and wasted hours driving indirect routes. And while this strategy did help her avoid new panic attacks, she also avoided overcoming her panic disorder. The treatment for the disorder required that she do the exact things she was afraid of doing, like driving on the freeway. To overcome panic, she needed to learn to cope not only with panic attacks themselves but, more importantly, with her fear of triggering a panic attack.

Indecisiveness

Indecisiveness is a special form of avoidance. In this case, rather than avoiding a task, you're avoiding making a decision. Sometimes, delaying decisions can be strategic and prudent: You may get more information later that will allow you to make a more informed choice, or you may get a better deal from a salesperson who is really motivated to sell to you. But when you have all the relevant information and choose not to make a decision, that's just decisional procrastination.

This type of indecisiveness is deeply rooted in avoidance. Postponing decisions means you avoid the responsibility and the aftermath of making a decision. You also get to avoid any anticipated regret or fear from making the "wrong" decision. No decision = no action = no change = no regret. Except, you end up regretting the indecisiveness and the time and opportunities wasted.

We trick ourselves into this type of avoidance by saying we just haven't made up our minds yet, when the reality is that a nondecision is really a decision in itself. If you haven't decided whether you want to break up with your boyfriend, each day you put off that decision is a day you're choosing to stay in the relationship. The nondecision to separate is a decision to remain together. Same thing with your goals: The nondecision about starting your next side hustle is a decision *not* to get started.

Dealing with Avoidance

Ultimately, the only way to overcome avoidance is to manage your feelings. If you want to stop procrastinating, you have to learn how to cope with the unpleasant emotions associated with doing a task, be willing to feel unpleasant emotions in the future, and accept the reality that you may sometimes regret your decisions. That last part might actually be the hardest. We want things to be perfect and we want to succeed, and sometimes, it feels like we can prevent failure by not taking action. But inaction is its own form of failure. When you don't take action, you deprive yourself of the opportunity to succeed, or at least to learn.

The following strategies are designed to help you take steps to manage those feelings that freeze you up and keep you from moving toward your goals.

We sometimes avoid tasks because we anticipate setbacks that we don't feel prepared to deal with. Many people avoid even trying to start a diet because they worry that there will be a day when they won't follow the diet and this will derail their entire effort. Why even bother if you won't make it to the end?

You can address this concern by anticipating potential setbacks and identifying the resources you have to respond to them. You probably have more resources than you realize: technology, money, people (e.g., people you know and trust or people who are experts in what you're trying to do), and your own knowledge from prior experience or education. But your greatest resource may be your *psychological capital.* Psychological capital is the amount of hope you have that you'll reach your goals, how well you bounce back from setbacks and adversity, and how optimistic and confident you are that you will succeed. When you are trying to commit to a new task but find yourself worrying about anticipated setbacks, remember your resources. Remind yourself that you know the steps to reach your goal, you have enough resilience to manage obstacles, and you believe in yourself enough to make this happen.

Once you realize how many resources you have, you will feel more prepared to tackle the task and you will be less likely to avoid it.

BREAK THE TASKS DOWN FURTHER

In chapter 7, you learned how to break your tasks down into individual components. One giant task can be intimidating, but several smaller tasks can feel more manageable. However, if you've broken down your task into more manageable steps but still feel overwhelmed, then your first step might still be too big. Break it down even further.

If a goal of "Clean the house" feels overwhelming, that's a cue to break it down into cleaning individual rooms. If "Clean the kitchen" is still overwhelming, then break that down, too. Now you're at "Wash the dishes." Still overwhelmed? Try "Wash one fork." Any step can be broken down until you're comfortable with it.

Try not to judge yourself for breaking tasks down into the tiniest of steps. It's better to take one tiny step forward and build momentum from there than to stay stuck. Even if all you do is wash one fork, that's still one more fork than was clean a few minutes ago. And you've shown yourself that you can deal with tough feelings, which builds confidence for the next task.

MONITOR YOUR NEGATIVE SELF-TALK

Have you ever waved at someone you know on the street, only to have them not wave back? What did you tell yourself after it happened? The story you tell yourself to explain any situation in your life is self-talk, and the kind of self-talk you use plays a major role in how you feel about and respond to situations. Positive self-talk will inspire you towards action, while negative self-talk will discourage you. If you tell yourself, "My friend probably didn't wave back because she's mad at me," you'll feel insecure and probably avoid waving to her in the future. If you tell yourself, "She might not have seen me," you might feel optimistic and decide to approach her to say hello.

The same thinking applies to difficult tasks you have been avoiding. If you tell yourself, "I can't do this," "I can't stand the way this makes me feel," or "I shouldn't have to do this," you'll feel discouraged, apprehensive, and aggravated and most likely avoid the task. But if you tell yourself, "This will be a challenge, but I can do hard things," you might feel more assured, determined, or confident. The encouraging thoughts lead to encouraging feelings, which help move us toward attempting difficult tasks.

When you're noticing negative self-talk, writing the thoughts down is a good idea. It's easier to see how unhelpful these thoughts are when they're written down. Writing also makes it easier to replace them with more helpful thoughts.

ASK YOURSELF THE MIRACLE QUESTION

Derived from solution-focused brief therapy (SFBT), the miracle question is a technique to use when you're feeling indecisive.

Suppose tonight while you are sleeping, a miracle occurs, and the decision you are avoiding has been made for you. You are asleep, so, of course, you don't know the miracle has happened. When you wake up the next morning, what would be the first sign that a miracle had occurred? Maybe you have been avoiding making a decision about which law school to attend. When you wake up the next morning, a miracle has happened: You're wearing pajamas with one school's insignia, there's a welcome packet from the school on your nightstand, and you've rented an apartment in that school's city. When you imagined it, which school did you see first and which city did you see yourself living in?

The miracle question helps us imagine what our lives would be like if the decision were already made. We can imagine the details of a life spent living with that decision. We can then use that information to determine which decision is the best for us. If one imagined miracle life feels more consistent with your goals or values than the other, that decision is likely the best.

ACKNOWLEDGE THE OUTCOMES OF INDECISIVENESS

Be honest with yourself about how indecisiveness is affecting you and your life. Often, we avoid making decisions because we don't want to limit our options. We think that if we choose one career path, we'll miss out on other opportunities, or if we choose one person to date, we might miss out on a better fit. It's true that sometimes committing to one path does limit other opportunities, but *not* committing can also limit us. Consider the effect of each decision, and also consider the effect of doing nothing, of *not* deciding. Another way to think about this is to ask yourself how you will feel about your indecisiveness in a week, a month, or a year. Will you be grateful you waited? Or would it have been better to have made a decision and moved forward with your life?

This can also be applied to tasks you are avoiding. Consider the effect of *doing* the task and also consider the effect of *not* doing the task. Ask yourself how you will feel in the future about avoiding the task, whether you'll be grateful you avoided it or if it would have been better to have committed to a course and moved forward. A classic example is exercise: What are the consequences of *not* exercising, and is it better to get started or to avoid it and be in the same place physically a year from now?

BE CONTENT WITH YOUR DECISIONS

One of the main drivers of indecisiveness is a fear of making the "wrong" choice or regretting your decisions later. The best way to deal with this? Accept that you aren't prophetic and that you have less information right now than you'll have in the future. Remember that the decision you're making now is the one that is best *given the available information.* Hindsight may make you wonder whether a different decision would have been better, but practice self-compassion by recognizing that you made a thoughtful decision with limited information. When you're making a tough choice, document your rationale for choosing this option over another so you can refer to your thought process in the future and recall what made this path the best at the time.

SOOTHE YOURSELF

We usually avoid tasks because we're trying to avoid how it feels to do them. If you're feeling distressed about making a therapy appointment, attending a social gathering, or asking for help, focus on soothing the emotional distress. Sure, one way to relieve the distress is to avoid the activity. But there's a reason you want to do this activity, so look for another soothing strategy you can use. Sing, hug yourself, laugh, or smile before you get started. Continue to soothe yourself while you're doing the task with those same strategies or by playing soothing music, lighting a scented candle, or drinking a soothing drink (e.g., hot chocolate, herbal tea). Be careful to choose soothing strategies that won't distract you from the task itself—you can get started on the task while listening to soothing music, but getting out your guitar might perpetuate your procrastination and avoidance.

Another strategy for soothing the emotional distress is to train yourself to relax. This strategy is most effective if you train yourself to relax on a regular basis. Practicing slow, deep breathing can quickly calm emotional distress and help you start a task you might be tempted to avoid.

Remember when your teacher would let you bring an index-card cheat sheet to your exam? Your handwriting was never tinier or neater than when you were cramming everything you could think of on that card. A coping card is the same thing, but for coping with difficult situations. Having this type of quick-reference guide ready can help us get through difficult feelings that make us want to abandon a task.

To start, grab an index card, tear a sheet of paper into quarters, or open a new note file in your phone. At the top, write the situation you're coping with. For example, "Coping Card for When I'm Doubting Myself." Then, list all the strategies you can use to cope with that situation. You might include strategies from this book or other strategies from your own research or personal experience. Next, list people you can contact for support, like a friend, relative, or mentor who can give you a little motivational boost. Finally, list three positive things you can focus on to help yourself cope (e.g., reasons you want to cope with the feeling rather than avoid it, an inspirational quote or idea, or something positive happening in your life).

If you notice yourself avoiding a task or a decision, examine whether it's due to an uncomfortable feeling. Then, follow the strategies on your coping card to manage the discomfort and keep going with the task.

The strategies in this chapter are not easy to do, and they certainly don't feel good. But they're incredibly important and can aid you in your journey to overcome procrastination and achieve your personal and professional goals. I hope you'll spend some extra time with these proven techniques—remember, the more you practice something, the easier it will become. Give yourself the opportunity to learn these strategies, put them into action, and feel how free your life becomes when avoidance and indecisiveness aren't holding you back.

Now that you've developed skills to get your tasks started, your next objective is to keep that momentum alive and follow through to the end. That's where we're headed next.

CHAPTER TEN

Follow Through

Once you've started a task, your next challenge is to follow it through to completion. Many factors can derail you, from distractibility to forgetfulness to difficulty recovering from setbacks. This is especially true for longer-term projects or multi-step tasks, which come with multiple opportunities to get off task. To maximize your ability to follow through, let's start by learning why consistent effort is so difficult and then examine some proven techniques to help you continue with a task.

After You Start

Follow-through is your ability to stick with an action or a task until it's finished. Madison had struggled with follow-through all her life. Her apartment was filled with half-completed projects: a shelf she purchased but never hung, a half-folded pile of clothes, brownie batter that sat in the fridge for weeks but never made it to the oven. Madison would start a project but then get distracted and simply never finish.

Follow-through can be particularly problematic for people who have ADHD, as neurologically based distractibility inhibits their ability to focus on a task long enough to complete it. But it's also an issue for people with depression, who run out of energy before they complete tasks, as well as people with anxiety, who have trouble coping with self-doubt and drop tasks out of worry that they won't do a good job. Nearly all of us can get derailed when we run into an unexpected problem we aren't sure how to solve.

Sustained Effort

One of the reasons it's so difficult to maintain consistent effort is that our brains have trouble remembering why we wanted to complete a particular task in the first place. The brain's number one priority is to conserve energy, so it will work really hard to talk us out of doing things that will cost us energy. This is why you've likely experienced random bursts of effort, commitment, or productivity when you remembered why a task mattered to you, followed by long periods of inactivity with low interest or motivation.

Consistent effort requires that you consistently feed your brain the fuel it needs (e.g., by eating healthy, exercising, taking breaks, etc.) and that you remind yourself why spending energy on this task matters.

A general principle for establishing consistency is to break larger tasks and goals into smaller, more manageable steps, and then schedule those steps regularly over a period of time. This type of planning and structure helps you sustain energy, which helps you sustain effort.

In addition to that foundation, try these other proven strategies for following through and completing the tasks you've started.

Sometimes, when we encounter an issue we hadn't anticipated—we run out of materials, we need help, we don't have enough time—our follow-through is compromised. Whenever our focus shifts from the task itself, we're at risk for becoming distracted and getting off task. Mitigate this risk by developing a plan that allows your task to flow as efficiently as possible, from beginning to end.

Making a plan starts with deciding which task you want to do. Once you've decided, consider all the steps necessary to complete the task, all the materials required, how much time it'll take, and any help you'll need. For example, before you start painting your house, decide what order you'll paint the rooms, the colors for each room, whether you'll ask anyone to help you paint, and what types of rollers or brushes you'll use. Write all this down so you won't have to make the same decisions twice.

By planning every step at once, you're lumping all the decision-making into a single unit—it's like buying in bulk. Decision-making takes a *lot* of mental energy, so limiting the number of decisions your brain has to make is a huge help and ensures you have the energy you need to actually complete the project. This strategy works best if you do it the night before you start the task. That way, your brain will have time to recover from decision fatigue while you sleep, and you'll be energized and ready to follow the plan when you wake up in the morning.

STRATEGIZE YOUR TIME

When you're making a plan, pay particular attention to how you're planning your time.

As we discussed in chapter 2, humans are pretty bad at estimating the time needed to complete a task. Consider giving yourself an extra five minutes for every 30 minutes you think you'll need, and then adjust accordingly. Having enough time will ensure that you're able to complete the work and follow through with what you started.

Also, consider how you will divide your time. Will you dedicate consistent time to the task until it is completed? Consistency requires a lot of sustained effort. Front-loading—spending a lot of time on the task in the beginning—sometimes leads to forgetting what the project is about as you go on. And rear-loading—focusing your time towards the end of the task—sometimes leads to inferior work or running out of time. Each approach has its challenges and can lead to problems with follow-through, so address those concerns in your plan.

Finally, consider planning larger chunks of time to complete projects. For some projects, two consecutive hours of work (with breaks!) can be much more helpful than 10 minutes here and there. When we're constantly switching back and forth between tasks, it's hard for our brains to stay focused. Longer periods of engagement with a single task can enhance progress.

PROBLEM-SOLVE SETBACKS

Inevitably, as you work towards your goal, you *will* run into unanticipated problems. Stopping to solve these problems can be distracting—or, even worse, it can make you feel so overwhelmed that you avoid solving them altogether and just quit. That's why it's so important to develop a strategy for addressing setbacks.

Problem-solving has five steps. The first is to identify the problem. This part might seem so simple that you're tempted to skip over it. But actually, identifying the problem can be surprisingly tricky. Maybe your goal is to remove the wallpaper in your bathroom, but it won't come off. Step one is to identify whether the problem is that the wallpaper isn't wet enough or that you haven't waited long enough for the water to penetrate the glue. Step two is to generate as many ideas as possible to solve the problem: Add more water with a sponge, a spray bottle, or a water-soaked paint roller, or even splash water on the walls from the shower. Don't censor yourself; writing down every idea, even the outrageous ones, will help your brain stay in the flow of generating ideas, making you more likely to stumble across a creative solution. Step three is where you'll eliminate the ideas that obviously won't work. Quickly weigh the pros and cons of the remaining solutions and choose one strategy to try first. Here's where you might realize that you already have a sponge handy and it'll get a lot of water on the wallpaper, though it might also make a mess. In step four, create a plan for implementing that idea and try it out: Soak your sponge and start rubbing the wallpaper. Finally, in step five, take a look at what you've tried and see if it worked. If you've solved the problem, great! But if not, go back to step three and try a different strategy.

Practicing this skill until it becomes second nature will help you become a pro at managing setbacks. The more confidence you have with solving these kinds of problems, the more likely you'll be to sustain your effort and follow through.

TALK YOURSELF THROUGH STUCK POINTS

Sometimes, when we get stuck, it kills our momentum. Maybe you're writing a paper and have run out of ideas, or maybe you're fixing an appliance and you can't figure out what the next step is. Getting stuck feels uncomfortable, and as soon as that discomfort shows up, your brain says, "Hey, maybe you should just play video games for a while until you think of something else to write." The next thing you know, you've been playing all night and your half-finished paper is due in an hour.

Get yourself unstuck by talking yourself through what you're doing. It's sometimes easier to generate ideas verbally than it is through writing, so if you're stuck on a paper, read aloud what you've written so far, then use dictation software to generate ideas about what might come next. If you don't have dictation software, use the audio recorder on your phone and then transcribe your ideas later. Or simply talk aloud to yourself to generate some momentum.

Use the same strategy for other stuck points. If you run into a snag while you're fixing the lawn mower, talk yourself through what you've done so far and what you know about lawn mower repair. Having this conversation aloud with yourself can help your brain connect pieces of information and generate new ideas to get you unstuck and help you follow through with the goal.

PLAN REWARDS

Many tasks we procrastinate are just boring—like studying for exams, filing taxes, paying bills, or opening the mail. Boredom is a risk factor for not following through. If an opportunity to do something more exciting or stimulating pops up while you're working on a boring task, you're liable to get distracted. You might promise yourself you'll come back to the boring task later, but that thought process perpetuates problems with follow-through. Instead, manage boredom-induced distractibility by planning a reward for completing the task.

Maybe the best reward for you is grabbing a couple of boxes of candy or microwave popcorn, renting a movie, and planning a stay-at-home movie night. Maybe it's treating yourself to a fancy coffee drink or allowing yourself a guilt-free soak in the bathtub with some candles and a magazine. The specific reward doesn't matter—only that it feels rewarding to you. Having something exciting to look forward to can help us persist through the boring discomfort of following through.

USE AN ACCOUNTABILITY PARTNER

An accountability partner is someone who checks in with you regularly and helps you stay committed to a goal. Knowing your accountability partner will ask you for an update each week helps you continue to follow through, even when you're tempted to give up or avoid. They help you maintain your motivation during the tough moments and ensure that you follow through to reach your goals.

Some things to keep in mind as you select and work with an accountability partner: Choose someone you trust to check on you consistently and call you out when you're off task. Work with your partner to specify what you want to accomplish and identify any rewards that might be appropriate if you're staying on task or reach your goal. Agree to check in with each other at a regular time and occasionally review your goal and your progress to make sure you haven't drifted off course.

SET INTERMEDIATE GOALS

It can be especially difficult to follow through with long-term projects that occur over several days, weeks, months, or years, such as learning a new language or musical instrument. Consequently, we can get distracted from our goal in favor of shorter-term or more urgent tasks or activities. But setting smaller, intermediate goals can make it easier to follow through with longer-term goals.

If you're learning to play the piano, you might set a goal to learn a Mozart piece by a particular date. This helps reduce the overwhelm that comes from focusing on a monumental goal. Smaller goals help you recognize that long-term projects are manageable when you focus on these intermediate objectives.

Set goals as often as necessary. If you're writing a book, you might have daily writing goals; if your goal is keeping in touch with friends, you might have weekly check-in goals. If your larger goal is saving for retirement, you might have monthly savings goals. Setting these goals and scheduling periodic check-ins with yourself to review your progress can help you follow through to completion.

ACCEPT "GOOD ENOUGH"

Perfectionism is one of the greatest threats to following through. We may get excited about a goal and get started on it, only to begin to worry about whether we're making mistakes or working hard enough. Those doubts create anxiety, which we avoid by disengaging from the task. Once disengaged, it's difficult to reengage and follow through.

Just because pursuing perfection is a possibility, that doesn't mean it is necessary, or even that it's preferable or advantageous. Confront your perfectionism and challenge yourself to adopt a "good enough" approach. I've noticed the phrase "good enough" seems to have a negative connotation—almost like the definition of "good enough" is "*not* good enough." It seems that we've equated "good enough" with "lazy" or "inadequate." But "good enough" means exactly what it says—good.

What counts as "good enough" depends on the task. If you're an accountant doing taxes or a surgeon performing a coronary bypass, "good enough" needs to basically be perfect. But if you're making a cake for your child's third birthday, finishing a workout, or trimming your hedges, "good enough" likely has an entirely different meaning.

Be clear with yourself about what is actually necessary, preferable, or advantageous with your particular task. And remember that perfection is an illusion. Don't let the pursuit of something fictitious be a roadblock for following through.

Now that you know how to follow through with the tasks you've started, there's just one more piece to the puzzle of overcoming procrastination: making sure you actually finish those tasks. This can be difficult if you're afraid of more responsibility, pressure, or expectations on the other side of success. But you've worked so hard—it's time to let yourself get to the finish line.

So, let's develop some strategies for finishing what you started.

CHAPTER ELEVEN

Finish What You Started

Procrastination is as much about finishing tasks as it is about starting them. While chapter 10 was about coping with distractibility and other factors that can keep us from *getting* to the finish line, this chapter is about actually *crossing* it. It's about managing the emotions and thoughts interfering with our ultimate success. By the time you've gotten to the end of a project, you've done a lot of hard work and proved how dedicated you are to your goal. But sometimes, fear can get in the way of putting on the final touches. In this chapter, we'll dive into those fears, and you'll learn proven strategies for facing both your fear of failure and fear of success.

Getting Over the Finish Line

Crossing the finish line can be difficult for just about anyone. As you come close to achieving your goal, you might experience perfectionism, which is associated with a fear of failure ("If I make a mistake, I'll be rejected"). Or you might feel imposter syndrome, which is associated with a fear of success ("If I succeed, they'll find out I'm a fraud"). Completing a project can also be tough for people with depression ("If I accomplish this, people will expect even more of me") or ADHD ("I'm not organized/focused/motivated enough to go to the next level if I succeed with this"). What each of these scenarios has in common is self-limiting beliefs—perceptions or assumptions that hold you back from reaching your potential.

When Jacob was in his early 20s, he went on a health kick. He ate well, exercised, and was the most confident he'd ever been in his body. While many people complimented his success, his closest friends and family mocked him for bringing healthy food to a pizza party and skipping a picnic to run a 5k race. Eventually, he started to feel alienated by his success and fell into a depression. Over the next decade, he regained the weight. During this time, he'd begin a new diet and fitness regimen in fits and starts, only to quit soon after. With therapy, he realized he was afraid that if he accomplished his health goals, he'd be alienated from his friends and family again. His fear of not being accepted was keeping him from accomplishing his own goals.

Fear of Success and Failure

Most people are afraid of failing. In fact, many of us have had the experience of being so convinced we'd fail at something, we didn't even try. But while being afraid of failure is normal, it can become a problem when it overrides your drive for success, keeps you from accomplishing your personal and professional goals, or prevents you from finishing a task with your best effort. Maybe you believe that, no matter how hard you try, your project will never meet your standards. You then ignore it for as long as possible and blame your flawed final product on the time crunch, not personal inadequacy.

The fear of failure is really grounded in a fear of being rejected, or at least not accepted. We equate self-acceptance and social acceptance with perfection and assume that if my *task* isn't good enough, then *I'm* not good enough.

A fear of failure is relatable, but it can be harder to understand why someone would be afraid of success. Even the people who *are* afraid of success don't understand it! Often, fear of success is more about the fear of what comes *after* the success than the success itself. Once you succeed with one thing, you may expect even more from yourself or believe that other people will expect even more. That constantly increasing pressure can be intimidating. Sometimes, a fear of success can come from uncertainty about what comes next. Some people are scared to graduate from college because then they'll have to establish a career. This can be daunting for someone who has self-limiting beliefs. Some people have experienced genuinely negative consequences due to their success—their parents mocked them for getting good grades at school or their coworkers abandoned them after they got promoted. Across the board, success means something will change, even if it's for the better. Change comes with uncertainty and with uncertainty comes anxiety, which we're motivated to avoid.

Crossing the finish line involves confronting these self-limiting beliefs, and that's where the following evidence-based strategies come in.

TALK TO YOURSELF WITH COMPASSION

Self-compassion involves offering kindness to relieve suffering. "Suffering" can be experienced on a deep level, like in cases of trauma, but it can also be part of ordinary experiences, like when you make a mistake. It's part of the normal human experience: Everyone suffers. That means that everyone benefits from self-compassion. Research shows that talking to ourselves with compassion (rather than criticism) decreases negative moods and increases motivation.

Fears related to failure might come in the form of self-criticism: "I'm sure I'll never get it right," "I might as well give up now," or "There's no point in even trying because it won't work out." And fears related to success might come in the form of self-doubt: "I'm not smart enough for this promotion," "I won't be able to keep this success streak going," or "People will find out I don't know what I'm doing."

When you have these types of thoughts, imagine what you would say to someone you care about in a similar situation. Your friend is doubting herself, despite being *so close* to accomplishing her goal, and you want to encourage her. Consider not just what you would say but also how you would say it. What words would you use? What advice would you give? And what tone of voice, facial expressions, or gestures would you use as you talked? Being able to speak to yourself with compassion, the way you would speak to a good friend, allows you to help yourself through an issue and actually take steps toward reaching your goals.

RESPOND TO SELF-CRITICISM

Self-critical thoughts can come in the form of name-calling (e.g., "I'm such an idiot") or other unhelpful or disparaging language (e.g., "I'm not good enough," "No one likes me," or "I can't do it"). These demoralizing thoughts keep us from working toward our goals. It's important to catch these thoughts and check them for accuracy. When you catch one of these self-critical thoughts, respond by thinking of two other thoughts, interpretations, or reactions you could have to the situation.

For example: You're starting a new healthy lifestyle. Your self-criticism says, "You'll do it for three weeks and then fail, like you always do." Now, consider additional thoughts, interpretations, or reactions you could have: "I'll get this perfectly from the start," "I might have some stumbling blocks, but I can ask my sister for encouragement or help if I need it," or "There will probably be days when I don't make it to the gym or eat well, but I'll need to remember that's a normal part of the journey." Not all of the new thoughts need to be realistic, or even true; the point is to show your brain that there are many ways to think about the situation, not just the one critical way that it immediately went to. Hopefully, though, you'll stumble across some thoughts that *are* more helpful, and you can carry them with you to cross the finish line.

CONSIDER THE EVIDENCE

If you are afraid of failure, consider whether the evidence supports the belief that you'll fail. Maybe you have a school project that you have been procrastinating. You're feeling intimidated and think you won't do a good job. In your past, you've rushed to complete these projects at the last minute, telling yourself it's better to fail because you ran out of time than because you aren't smart enough. Confront those thoughts and see if the evidence supports them. First, generate evidence that proves you'll fail: You have had some trouble mastering the material recently, and you aren't really sure what the professor is looking for in this project. Now, generate evidence that shows you *won't* fail: You've never actually failed a project before, you have some ideas for the project, and you could ask for more information at your professor's office hours this week.

Often, there is *some* truth to our fears—we've had some life experience that's made us develop this fear, or there's some legitimate probability that what we fear could happen. It's also important to recognize there is contradictory evidence—we've had many more life experiences that contradict what the fear is telling us, and there's a difference between something being *possible* and something being *probable*. Lay out *all* the evidence, not just the evidence that supports your fear. That way, you can make a more balanced and reliable assessment of whether you want to behave as if the fear is true or whether you want to face your fears.

IMAGINE YOURSELF COPING

If fear of success or fear of failure is holding you back from finishing a task, project, or goal, you may notice flashes of images in your mind—a picture of yourself freezing in a job interview, an image of yourself getting fired, or a visual of your classmates laughing at you. If these images don't appear automatically, generate them for yourself by imagining something you fear will happen if you complete your goal.

Next, imagine yourself *coping* with that feared outcome. Imagine what you would do if you froze in a job interview. Would you just sit there indefinitely, until someone called a paramedic to come wheel you out? Most likely not. How would you cope? Maybe you'd ask the interviewer to repeat the question, ask for a break, make a joke, or maybe one of the interviewers would ask if you needed some water. Imagine what would come *after* you began to cope. Imagining yourself coping with success or failure can show you that you are more capable of navigating stressors than your anxiety would lead you to believe.

APPRECIATE THE POSITIVES OF SUCCESS

Success isn't usually entirely positive—new expectations develop when you succeed, as do new issues and problems. The uncertainty of what can follow success sometimes prevents us from crossing the finish line. To manage this, make a list of the lessons you would learn from success. Most likely, you will learn new skills, meet new people to mentor you or help with your next adventure, and build confidence to manage adversity (in other words, build psychological capital, like we discussed in chapter 9). As you create your list, consider what success would do for you personally. You'd never have to regret or wonder "what if," you'd develop a sense of progression rather than stagnation, and you'd overcome some personal insecurity. Then, compare this list of the "positives of success" to your concerns or fears about success. Decide which set of outcomes is most consistent with your goals. Would you rather continue to generate doubt and fear by holding yourself back? Or would you prefer to build confidence and courage by pursuing a challenge?

USE A REVERSE DEADLINE

You're familiar with regular deadlines, but you may not have heard of a reverse deadline. A reverse deadline is an amount of time you commit to trying something before you quit. Say you want to learn a computer programming language, but frustration and a fear of never becoming proficient are holding you back. Try setting a reverse deadline for yourself that includes an amount of time you are willing to commit to practicing coding—maybe 30 minutes a day, or an hour a week. This type of reverse deadline helps us continue to move towards our goals rather than feel paralyzed by fears, while also making the commitment seem more manageable. Another application of this strategy is to commit to trying a new skill for six months or one year, to allow yourself a realistic opportunity to learn it before deciding you'll never be good at it.

CONNECT THE TASK TO YOUR GOALS

When we're wrapped up in the stress about an individual task, it's easy to lose sight of the greater importance of our work. Typically, any task, activity, or project is part of a larger goal: Completing this physics project is part of your larger goal of completing your degree, which contributes to your larger goal of supporting yourself independently. Once you remember the greater purpose, it's easier to challenge yourself to overcome the fears that might hold you back.

Try writing down three reasons it's important to you to complete the task. Consider how quitting or finishing would impact your life goals. Tackling this physics project will (1) help me prepare for the exam, (2) make me more competitive for med school, and (3) give me an opportunity to show myself that I can do hard things. Often, this exercise helps us realize that following through with a task will take us closer toward our goals, whereas quitting will keep us stuck. That may be the extra push you need to finish what you started.

USE POSITIVE AFFIRMATIONS

Positive affirmations are statements or mantras designed to provide encouragement, and research shows that they enhance confidence (Hatzigeorgiadis, Zourbanos, Mpoumpaki, and Theodorakis, 2009). Choose affirmations that address your doubts and provide encouragement. For example, if you are afraid of failing, you might choose affirmations like "Done is better than perfect," "Action is better than perfection," or "Challenges are opportunities to grow." Or if a fear of success is holding you back, you might benefit from affirmations like "My actions are taking me closer to my goals," "I am capable of troubleshooting obstacles," or "I am ready." Inspirational quotes, religious scripture, and advice from your mentors are all great sources of positive affirmations. Keep track of your favorite mantras on your coping cards (chapter 9, see page 104). Remember, fear is only a feeling—it can't hold you back.

Once you've dedicated your time and effort to getting a task started and managed to stay focused on it, you want to put a rubber stamp on it and mark it "DONE." The strategies in this chapter are all about helping you reap the rewards of your hard work by finishing what you started. Use these strategies to keep your self-limiting beliefs from holding you back. You've crossed the finish line of this chapter, and you're almost at the end of this book. Now, let's tie this all together.

Conclusion

Keep Working at It

Congratulations! You've finished this book, and that's an amazing accomplishment! You've put in a ton of work determining what caused your procrastination, which types of procrastination you struggle with the most, and which strategies will be most helpful for you. And you've discovered that overcoming procrastination is about two main things: feelings and motivation.

The idea of having to do unpleasant tasks is so aversive that we procrastinate to relieve the discomfort. But it's not the discomfort itself that's the issue; it's how we *react behaviorally* to the discomfort. Anxiety, insecurity, boredom, and frustration aren't harmful—they're just uncomfortable. Choosing healthy strategies to respond to those feelings is a major factor in overcoming procrastination. When you commit to approaching rather than avoiding what's making you stressed or uncomfortable, you can conquer the self-limiting beliefs and behaviors that have sabotaged your prior success.

We sabotage ourselves by believing we need to be motivated to take action. But your life experience will prove this is not true. Consider all the things you do without motivation—untangling your jewelry, unpacking your suitcase, going to work every day. The truth is that *action* leads to *motivation*, not the other way around. Promise yourself that even if you're not feeling up to it, don't think you have enough energy, or you just plain don't want to do it, you will show up and give it a good effort anyway. When you start with action, your success will follow. Momentum is a far more powerful force than motivation, so focus on action.

One of the greatest mistakes people make in reading personal growth or self-development literature is stopping at the end of the book. But this is just the beginning! You know everything you need to overcome your procrastination, but now is the time to put it into action. This part is just as important as the parts you've already read. Without action, the effort you've already dedicated to this process will be ineffective.

Uncertainty about what life after procrastination looks like might hold you back from following through with the action. Will you just become a boring cog who's always busy with "productive" projects and never has any fun? Take a few moments now to imagine what your life would look like if you didn't struggle with procrastination. What opportunities would open up? How would you make sure there's still time for fun? How would you navigate the change? Think it through so the fear of the uncertainty doesn't hold you back from achieving success.

Remember that list you made of reasons you wanted to finish this book? Take a look at it now. *Those* are the reasons it's important to continue your focus. Don't just use the strategies in this book to get things done—use them to help yourself follow through and cross the finish line with overcoming your procrastination itself. This is your chance to choose yourself, to make the hard choices and take the tough actions to finally accomplish your goals. You can do it.

Resources

Workbooks

Centre for Clinical Interventions
The Centre for Clinical Interventions is a specialized clinical psychology service in the Department of Health in Western Australia. You can access a seven-module procrastination workbook on their website that will help you outline your procrastination cycle and work through the thoughts, behaviors, and feelings that keep procrastination alive. They also have workbooks for managing some other issues that might be perpetuating your procrastination, like perfectionism or trouble tolerating discomfort. You can access the materials at CCI.Health.WA.gov.au/Resources/Looking-After-Yourself.

Podcasts

***ADDitude* Magazine's *ADHD Experts* Podcast**
For people whose procrastination is specifically associated with ADHD, *ADDitude* Magazine's *ADHD Experts* Podcast, in which leading researchers and other ADHD experts answer common questions about ADHD, is a helpful resource.

iProcrastinate
The *iProcrastinate* podcast is no longer in production, but 12 years of prior podcast episodes are available. Topics include why procrastination occurs and strategies for overcoming it.

The Joy of Procrastination
Hosts Dean Jackson and Dan Sullivan produce a biweekly podcast focused on reducing shame about procrastination and sharing strategies and motivation for overcoming it.

Websites

ADDitude Magazine

ADDitude Magazine is a leading source of information about ADD and ADHD. Its scientific advisory board includes some of the top psychologists, psychiatrists, and researchers in the country. You'll find free symptom tests, mindfulness exercises, and practical guides (like "How to Tidy Up Your Home Like a Pro") in addition to a magazine, webinars, e-books, and a store full of products specifically geared toward people with ADHD. It's a haven of resources. Get started at ADDitudeMag.com.

Procrastination Coach

Procrastination Coach, organized by psychologist Dr. Christine Li, includes free and paid procrastination resources. Access her materials at ProcrastinationCoach.com.

Books

Changing for Good: A Revolutionary Six-Stage Program for Overcoming Bad Habits and Moving Your Life Positively Forward **by James O. Prochaska, John C. Norcross, and Carlo C. DiClemente**

This book was written by three top psychologists who research how to overcome bad habits. They understand that building healthy habits doesn't come from luck or willpower, so this book is about their evidence-based process for actually making your new procrastination-busting habits stick.

Getting Things Done with Adult ADHD **by the Editors of *ADDitude* Magazine**

If you need more procrastination-fighting strategies specifically for ADHD-driven procrastination, this book is a great resource, filled with strategies for staying focused and overcoming procrastination. It's produced by *ADDitude* Magazine, one of the top resources for information and resources for ADHD.

Apps

The list of apps that can help you overcome procrastination is nearly endless, so experiment and find what works best for you. Here are some of my favorites.

BlockSite

BlockSite is another app- and website-blocker that reduces distractions.

Forest

Forest is an app that helps you stay focused. When you decide you want to stay focused, you plant a tree in the app. Your tree grows as you stay focused and dies if you get distracted.

Freedom

Freedom is an app- and website-blocker that reduces distractions.

RescueTime

RescueTime tracks the time you spend on apps, websites, and documents, so you'll know where your time is going. You can also set up alerts to stop working, which is helpful for people who have trouble knowing when to stop.

Simple Habit

Simple Habit is a meditation app designed for busy people who want the benefits of meditation (like reduced anxiety, improved focus, and better sleep) without dedicating themselves to a full-on meditation practice. It's great for people who need an extra boost for the strategies discussed in chapters 9 and 11.

Strict Workflow

Strict Workflow uses timers to encourage you take regular breaks while you're working, so you can refresh your attention and stay on task.

Todoist

Todoist is a to-do list app that keeps track of all your tasks, projects, and goals in a single place. It helps you get more focused and organized by getting all that information out of your head. It's great for people who need an extra boost for the strategies discussed in chapters 5 and 7.

Online Communities

ADDitude

The online community at ADDitude includes adults with ADD or ADHD supporting each other with personal experience and practical tips for managing their symptoms, including procrastination. Join the discussion at ADDitude Mag.com/forums.

How to ADHD

Jessica McCabe who has been diagnosed with ADHD, has a YouTube channel (How to ADHD) and TED Talks about living with ADHD ("Failing at Normal: An ADHD Success Story"; "This Is What It's Really Like to Live with ADHD").

Reddit Procrastinationism Group

This subreddit offers support and guidance from a community of procrastinators: Reddit.com/r/procrastinationism.

TED Talks

Laura Vanderkam: "How to Gain Control of Your Free Time"

Laura Vanderkam is a time-management expert who provides strategies to help you find more free time for the things that matter most. Watch here: TED.com/talks/laura_vanderkam_how_to_gain_control_of_your_free_time.

Tim Urban: "Inside the Mind of a Master Procrastinator"

Tim Urban uses humor to explain what keeps us stuck in the cycle of procrastination and how to get out of it. Watch here: TED.com/talks/tim_urban_inside_the_mind_of_a_master_procrastinator.

References

Baumeister, R. F. 2016. "Toward a General Theory of Motivation: Problems, Challenges, Opportunities, and the Big Picture." *Motivation and Emotion 40*(1), 1–10.

Bovend'Eerdt, T. J. H., Botell, R. E., and Wade, D. T. 2009. "Writing SMART Rehabilitation Goals and Achieving Goal Attainment Scaling: A Practical Guide." *Clinical Rehabilitation 23*(4), 352–361.

Briody, R. 1980. "An Exploratory Study of Procrastination." *Dissertation Abstracts International Section A: Humanities and Social Sciences 41*(2-A), 590.

Bunce, D. M., Flens, E. A., and Neiles, K. Y. 2010. "How Long Can Students Pay Attention in Class? A Study of Student Attention Decline Using Clickers." *Journal of Chemical Education 87*(12), 1438–1443.

Carney, D. R., Cuddy, A. J. C., and Yap, A. J. 2010. "Power Posing: Brief Nonverbal Displays Affect Neuroendocrine Levels and Risk Tolerance." *Psychological Science 21*(10), 1363–1368.

Chu, A. H. C., and Choi, J. N. 2005. "Rethinking Procrastination: Positive Effects of 'Active' Procrastination Behavior on Attitudes and Performance." *The Journal of Social Psychology 145*(3), 245–264.

Clancy, J. 1961. "Procrastination: A Defense Against Sobriety." *Quarterly Journal of Studies on Alcohol 22*(2), 269–276.

Credé, M., and Phillips, L. A. 2017. "Revisiting the Power Pose Effect: How Robust are the Results Reported by Carney, Cuddy, and Yap (2010) to Data Analytic Decisions?" *Social Psychological and Personality Science 8*(5), 493–499.

Dalton, B. H., and Behm, D. G. 2007. "Effects of Noise and Music on Human and Task Performance: A Systematic Review." *Occupational Ergonomics* 7(3), 143–152.

Ferrari, J. R. 2001. "Procrastination as Self-Regulation Failure of Performance: Effects of Cognitive Load, Self-Awareness, and Time Limits on 'Working Best Under Pressure.'" *European Journal of Personality* 15(5), 391–406.

Harriott, J., and Ferrari, J. R. 1996. "Prevalence of Procrastination Among Samples of Adults." *Psychological Reports* 78(2), 611–616.

Hatzigeorgiadis, A., Zourbanos, N., Mpoumpaki, S., and Theodorakis, Y. 2009. "Mechanisms Underlying the Self-Talk–Performance Relationship: The Effects of Motivational Self-Talk on Self-Confidence and Anxiety." *Psychology of Sport and Exercise* 10(1), 186–192.

Helps, S. K., Bamford, S., Sonuga-Barke, E. J. S., and Söderlund, G. B. W. 2014. "Different Effects of Adding White Noise on Cognitive Performance of Sub-, Normal and Super-Attentive School Children." *PLOS ONE* 9(11), e112768.

Hershfield, H. E. 2011. "Future Self-Continuity: How Conceptions of the Future Self Transform Intertemporal Choice." *Annals of the New York Academy of Sciences* 1235(1), 30–43.

Jong, P. D., and Berg, I. K. 2002. *Interviewing for Solutions.* 2nd ed. Pacific Grove, CA: Brooks/Cole.

Karch, D., Albers, L., Renner, G., Lichtenauer, N., and von Kries, R. 2013. "The Efficacy of Cognitive Training Programs in Children and Adolescents: A Meta-Analysis." *Deutsches Ärzteblatt International* 110(39), 643–652.

Kasper, G. "Tax Procrastination: Survey Finds 29% Have Yet to Begin Taxes." March 30, 2004. PRWeb.com/releases/2004/3/prweb114250.htm.

Kraus, J., and Porubanová, M. 2015. "The Effect of Binaural Beats on Working Memory Capacity." *Studia Psychologica 57*(2), 135–145.

Lally, P., van Jaarsveld, C. H. M., Potts, H. W. W., and Wardle, J. 2010. "How Are Habits Formed: Modelling Habit Formation in the Real World." *European Journal of Social Psychology 40*(6), 998–1009.

Mazur, J. E. 1996. "Procrastination by Pigeons: Preference for Larger, More Delayed Work Requirements." *Journal of the Experimental Analysis of Behavior 65*(1), 159–171.

McCloskey, J. D. "Finally, My Thesis on Academic Procrastination." Master's thesis, University of Texas at Arlington, December 2011. ProQuest (UMI No. 1506326).

O'Brien, W. K. "Applying the Transtheoretical Model to Academic Procrastination." Doctoral dissertation, University of Houston, 2000. ProQuest (UMI No. 3032320).

Pychyl, T. A., Lee, J. M., Thibodeau, R., and Blunt, A. 2000. "Five Days of Emotion: An Experience Sampling Study of Undergraduate Student Procrastination." *Journal of Social Behavior and Personality 15*(5), 239–254.

Sprich, S. E., Knouse, L. E., Cooper-Vince, C., Burbridge, J., and Safren, S. A. 2012. "Description and Demonstration of CBT for ADHD in Adults." *Cognitive and Behavioral Practice 17*(1), 9–15.

Steel, P. 2007. "The Nature of Procrastination: A Meta-Analytic and Theoretical Review of Quintessential Self-Regulatory Failure." *Psychological Bulletin 133*(1), 65–94.

Steel, P. 2010. "Arousal, Avoidant and Decisional Procrastinators: Do They Exist?" *Personality and Individual Differences 48*(8), 926–934.

Stephens, R. S., Roffman, R. A., and Curtin, L. 2000. "Comparison of Extended Versus Brief Treatments for Marijuana Use." *Journal of Consulting and Clinical Psychology 68*(5), 898–908.

Tuckman, B. W. 1991. "The Development and Concurrent Validity of the Procrastination Scale." *Educational and Psychological Measurement 51*(2), 473–480.

Valdez P. 2019. "Circadian Rhythms in Attention." *The Yale Journal of Biology and Medicine 92*(1), 81–92.

Yockey, R. D. 2016. "Validation of the Short Form of the Academic Procrastination Scale." *Psychological Reports 118*(1), 171–179.

Zhang, S., Becker, B., Chen, Q., and Feng, T. 2019. "Insufficient Task-Outcome Association Promotes Task Procrastination through a Decrease of Hippocampal–Striatal Interaction." *Human Brain Mapping 40*(2), 597–607.

Zhang, W., Wang, X., and Feng, T. 2016. "Identifying the Neural Substrates of Procrastination: A Resting-State fMRI Study." *Scientific Reports 6*(1), 1–7.

Index

Mental health conditions (*continued*)

Attention-Deficit/Hyperactivity
Disorder (ADHD), 30–31
as a cause of procrastination, 29, 41
consequences of procrastination
for, 22–23
depression, 31–32
imposter syndrome, 39–40
perfectionism, 37–39
self-esteem/self-confidence, 35–37
Miracle questions, 101–102
Momentum, 83
Motivation, 14, 69–76, 122

N

Neuroscience, 25

O

Organization, 94

P

Perfectionism, 37–39, 113
Physical health consequences, 22–23
Planning, 109
Positive affirmations, 121
Prefrontal cortex, 25
Prioritizing, 59–66
Problem-solving, 110–111
Procrastination
active, 6
causes of, 14–19
chronic, 9
consequences of, 8, 22–25
as a cycle, 26–27
defined, 4–5
myths about, 20–21
passive, 5–6
prevalence of, 6–7

questionnaire, 10
root causes of, 50
Procrastination defense, 35
Psychological capital, 100
Psychology, 11, 50

Q

Quality of life, prioritizing by, 65–66

R

Regrets, 85
Relationship consequences, 24
"Remember, then do" strategy, 73
Resources, identifying, 100
Reverse deadlines, 120
Rewards, 55–56, 111–112
Routines, 56

S

Schedules, 82–83
Self-awareness, 52
Self-compassion, 51, 117–118
Self-confidence, 35–37
Self-control, 14
Self-criticism, 117–118
Self-esteem, 35–37
Self-monitoring, 14
Self-soothing, 103
Self-talk, 101, 118
SMART goals, 54
Solution-focused brief therapy (SFBT), 101
Sound, 92
Starting tasks, 79–85
Stress, 22–23
Structure, 56
Stuck points, 111
Success, fear of, 117, 119–120
Suffering, 117

Acknowledgments

Not long ago, while we were riding in the car, my mother abruptly exclaimed, "You should write a book!" Well, here it is, Mom! To my parents, thank you for inspiring me to write this book. From reading nearly everything I've ever written to supporting my decision to move all the way to Nebraska to become a psychologist, your sacrifices have allowed me to grow. And to my loving husband, thank you for your unwavering confidence in me. You've never doubted me, even when I impulsively started a psychology blog or said I was going to write a book. Your faith in me is my primary motivation. Thank you, dear.

About the Author

 **Hayden Finch**'s journey to become a licensed clinical psychologist started when she was a nine-year-old on the playground with her friends at recess. Her friends would come to her with their fourth-grade problems: Gross Bobby said he likes me. I got in trouble for talking in class too much. I just realized I put my underwear on backward today. These were serious issues, and they'd work through them together.

A decade later, Hayden landed at Duke University, pursuing a bachelor's degree in psychology. While there, she volunteered at a state psychiatric hospital, working with people with the most severe and persistent mental illnesses. She also worked in a cognitive psychology laboratory, researching how memory works and how people learn new information. She was fascinated.

She couldn't get enough psychology, so ultimately, she ended up in a doctoral program in Nebraska. Like you, she didn't *really* know where Nebraska was, and there sure wasn't any reason to *choose* to move there. Except for Dr. Will Spaulding. He runs a laboratory there studying how people with severe and persistent mental illnesses understand others and interpersonal relationships, and she just *had* to get her hands dirty with that. She spent several years in Nebraska training with Dr. Spaulding, developing outpatient and residential treatment programs for people with these mental illnesses, and getting involved in mental health policy and legislation advocacy.

The last step to completing her PhD in clinical psychology was a full-year stint at the Veterans Administration. She grew up in a military town and always had a desire to give back to military members, so training at the VA was an amazing opportunity to combine her commitment to veterans with her passion for mental health.

Now, she is Dr. Hayden Finch, a licensed clinical psychologist. She owns a mental health clinic, where she works every day with people just like you: people who have big goals for themselves but sometimes run into some hiccups while turning those dreams into reality. She teaches her clients techniques, skills, and information from cognitive behavioral therapy and other treatments rooted in psychological science. Together, they work to overcome the symptoms and side effects of depression, anxiety, ADHD, and a range of other mental health conditions. It's a lot like sitting on the playground in fourth grade, except with a few more decades of life experience, a lot more education, and lives and problems that are much more consequential.

Outside the office, you'll find Dr. Finch with her husband and two dogs, Ava and Bailey. Aside from her family and psychology, her favorite things in life are Dairy Queen Chocolate Xtreme Blizzards, dogs with sandy noses, and waterslides . . . because she's basically still a fourth-grader at heart.